X-treme cuisine

AN ADRENALINE-CHARGED COOKBOOK FOR THE YOUNG AT HEART

blank or whatever

X-treme cuisine

AN ADRENALINE-CHARGED COOKBOOK FOR THE YOUNG AT HEART

with Robert Earl

HarperEntertainment

An Imprint of HarperCollins*Publishers*

X-TREME CUISINE. Copyright © 2002 by Robert Earl Wells IV.
All rights reserved. Printed in the United States of America. No part of this
book may be used or reproduced in any manner whatsoever without written
permission except in the case of brief quotations embodied in critical articles
and reviews. For information address HarperCollins Publishers Inc., 10 East
53rd Street, New York, NY 10022.

HarperCollins books may be purchased for educational,
business, or sales promotional use. For information please write:
Special Markets Department, HarperCollins Publishers Inc., 10 East 53rd Street,
New York, NY 10022.

FIRST EDITION

Designed by Peter Morris, Smashing Designs; Robert Earl; and Amy Anderson

Printed on acid-free paper

Library of Congress Cataloging-in-Publication Data
Earl, Robert.
      X-treme cuisine: an adrenaline-charged cookbook for
   the young at heart / with Robert Earl.—1st ed.
         p. cm.
      ISBN 0-06-009413-3 (hc: alk. paper)   1. Cookery. I. Title.

TX652 .E296 2002
641.5—dc21   2002068832

02 03 04 05 06 RRD 10 9 8 7 6 5 4 3 2 1

dedication

To my X-wife, Lisa Katrin Tuttle, for her years of tireless dedication spent training and turning a caveman into a gentleman—or something close to a gentleman. Also to my grandpa Eddie who, although I didn't appreciate it at the time, gave me the best etiquette tip ever. "Robby," he said, "don't be fartin' in front of the ladies," just after I let a ripper go in the backseat of his car at age twelve. And, of course, my number one fan— Miss West Palm Beach 1942, Inez L. Wells (Himer).

Scallops, white wine beurre-blanc sauce reduction with red food coloring.

Bon appétit, mes amis.

—Robert Earl

blank

contents

contents

contents

blank

acknowledgments

To those who
believe the speed of
light travels at
186,000 miles per
second and this
thought alone can
fill a moment of
silence for hours.
—Robert Earl

Please drive safely.

I AM CORN HEAR ME ROAR

They may be your heroes, they may be major celebrities, but everybody in this book—at one time or another—has been in the same spot you are: absolutely clueless about cooking and how to act respectable at the dinner table. Whether out on the road, staying with friends, or hunkerin' down with the family, these athletes have tweaked and perfected at least one signature dish to go along with their bag of big air tricks. And now, for the first time, all the epicurean secrets of the world's greatest action-sports athletes and personalities are out.

This book is a little Martha, a little Wolfgang, a pinch of Miss Manners, and a whole lotta me, taking wacked little tidbits that can actually help with your overall sweetness factor.

But pulling off a big move in the kitchen is useless unless you display a little showmanship at the table, on the beach, or at a party. That's right: you've got to have at least a little etiquette in your back pocket. You've got to know when to pull out the big fork and when to use the small one, what to do with your napkin when you leave the table, and what about that soup spoon parallelism. Surfing, skating, snowboarding, skiing, riding a bike, a MotoX bike, eating and its presentation and delivery: you've got it all right here, one-stop shopping on how to be an extreme diner.

So head into the kitchen or just sit back, relax, and keep reading. I've pulled together some of the world's greatest athletes and action-sports players and personalities to give you their recipes, the ultra-inside scoop on their lives, etiquette tips (that some of them have never actually learned), and some sport-specific tips straight from the school of hard knocks.

Oh, and a bunch of other useless crap.

Bon appétit,

Robert Earl

blank

Foreword

Robert Earl is a culinary vanguard, earning the title through years of experience and plenty of bad food (this means fast food and food on the road, like Ding Dongs, Twinkies, and Taco Bell). Being a skate-tour veteran makes him a food connoisseur by default. Often, a motivating factor for our tours, sometimes even ahead of the skating itself, is when and where to have our next meal. Frequency is a major concern—the more often we eat, the better. Partially because of our skewed priorities on the road, Robert Earl has eaten at the finest restaurants—the kind that require background checks just to get reservations—but he can also keep it real with the occasional fast-food "run for the border" while traveling on our often smelly, sometimes low-budget, and always disorganized skate safari buses. Some of my fondest memories of the vast spectrum of our gastronomical travels include calamari salads at Asia de Cuba in Hollywood, robotic drink servers at Yo! Sushi in London, daily ham-and-cheese baguettes in Paris, huge lobsters that required donning bibs in Newport, RI, PB&J's in the middle of nowhere while on the highway in the Jones Soda RV, the finest ribs in Texas, spicy rock shrimp at Nobu in NYC, Rob and SPF arriving in drag to an Indian place in Virginia, peanut fights in Oregon, and Robert Earl getting violently sick after too much foie gras in SF. These were all stepping stones in making Robert Earl a Jedi of Chichi Cuisine.

I can't say he's a world-renowned master chef, but he knows what tastes good, and thankfully he's employed the help of more experienced chefs to bring you the best of action-sports diets. Bon appétit!

Tony Hawk

WHITE TRASH CASSEROLE

1 BAG POTATO CHIPS (preferably BAR-B-QUE)
FLAVORED
1 PACKAGE MACARONI + CHEESE
1 CAN OF BAKED BEANS OR CHILI
IT DOESN'T get ANY Simpler THAN THIS:
COOK THE MACARONI + cheese
COOK THE BEANS OR CHILI
LINE A PLATE W/ A HEALTHY HEAPING
PORTION OF CHIPS...
ADD THE MACARONI + cheese.
ADD THE BEANS OR CHILI
MIX TOGETHER AND EITHER EAT W/ YOUR HANDS
LIKE NACHOS OR USE A FORK.
— Mike V.

mike valley: white trash casserole

Mike, what's the history of this culinary insanity? Where'd it come from?
It was originally invented in junior high school. I was so inspired after taking Home Economics that for a while I worked just as hard at cooking as I did at skating. At the time, I considered myself a master chef, but obviously, skating won out. I'm glad too, I'd probably be really fat right now f I'd gone the whole chef route.

And skating has been a beautiful experience, so I highly recommend it, just like I recommend my white trash casserole. This JHS recipe was eventually perfected while camping in Alaska with my friend Jason in 1997. That's what this thing really is—an outdoor camping recipe. It's something to eat while sitting around a campfire with your friends.

Got an etiquette tip for us?
Pick up the check every now and then.

What's your favorite grub?
I was a vegetarian for nearly ten years, and in that time I worked up quite an appetite for meat. These days I prefer a good steak or some sushi—about as far from a vegetarian diet as you can imagine.

Do you eat anything special before an event?
I eat light if at all, and I definitely stay away from the white trash. I always eat some type of protein bar, though. Sponsors, anyone?

1

Super soul rider #1 lives the life that every surfer dreams of. He does what he wants, when he wants. One night it's playing with his band Sunchild, the next it's hopping off to the Islands to film a video with Slater, Curren, or some other heavyweights, and the next it's searching out a vintage Gibson to round out his guitar collection.

He might love the hot wings at Santori's in Mission Viejo when he and the band are playing, but for *X-treme Cuisine* he pulled out his all-time favorite recipe, "Petra's Stir-fry Chicken Vegetable Curry."

DONAVON FRANKENREI

Where'd it come from?
I've found pieces of recipes here and there in cookbooks, included stuff from friends and years of exotic travel, but I've always found adding some of my own elements to be refreshing and fun. This is not your normal stir-fry. It's spicy and the presentation is absolutely beautiful.

Who did you make it for first?
For my wife back before she was my wife. So I guess it worked since we're now married, married, married! I was a bit nervous since it was the first time I'd ever cooked in my life. I guess I figured I better start sometime, so I really went for something exotic and spicy to really set the mood. Man, did it turn out good.

Random info
Lubrication, plain and simple: Whoever you're cooking for (as long as they're over twenty-one), make sure they're comfortable and have a good cocktail in their hands to set the mood and ensure the meal goes down smoothly. Even if you're not the master chef and you've burned a dish or two, everybody will manage to have a great time if you keep them gently lubricated.

Favorite food?
Mexican. You can't beat it. Oh, and of course anything prepared by my lovely wife.

Anything special to eat before an event?
I'm pretty lucky about the whole event thing. I don't really have to do them. But when those days come up and I jump in an early morning heat, I make sure that I don't eat much.

Donavon in search of the holy wok

Dono and Petra, lovebirds

Getting ready for the road with Sunchild

ter: Petra's stir-fry chicken vegetable curry

ingredients

2 tablespoons peanut oil
3 garlic cloves, minced
2 teaspoons ginger, finely chopped
1 red onion, finely chopped
1 pound boneless, skinless chicken breasts cut into
   1-inch chunks
3 tablespoons soy sauce
2 to 3 tablespoons curry powder or paste
   (paste is usually better)
1 cup water
1 cup chicken stock
2 red potatoes cut into 3/4-inch cubes
   (leave the skin on)
2 peeled carrots cut into 2-inch pieces

what to do

Warm the oil in a wok or frying pan (a wok is usually better) until it is very, very hot, but not quite boiling. Add the garlic, ginger, and onion. Stir and cook for approximately 3 minutes or until everything is softened up. Add the chicken chunks and cook until the chicken is white all the way through (you shouldn't see any pink in the chicken). Once properly cooked, put the chicken-chunk mix into a separate bowl for later use.

Now, in the wok, add the soy sauce, curry, water, stock, potatoes, and carrots. Bring it to a simmer, then reduce the heat and cook for 15 minutes. Keep covered and give it a little stir every 5 minutes.

After 15 minutes, add the chicken-chunk mix you prepared earlier. Cook for roughly another 10 minutes.

Bonus Love Song

"ON MY MIND"

VERSE 1...
OH BABY LETS GET DOWN toNite
EVER time WE DO Just feels so right
lets go sit underneath that willow tree.
OH BABY JUST A you AND mE....

CHORS... EVEN though I cant see you All the time
I got to let you know your on my mind

VERSE 2... You take those duds and make A sunny day
I Love to watch you do it, Just your own way
Lets go sit underneath that moonlight
OH BABY girl I'll hold you tight....

CHORS... EVEN though I cant see you All the time
I got to let you know your on my mind.

Chors out... ON my mind, on my mind again
on my mind, on my mind Again....
well I got to let you know,
that I will never let you go.....
"Never let you go..... Love,
Donavon Frankenreiter

At that point, the sauce will begin to thicken. Be sure to taste it during this time because it's your big chance to make any adjustments.

From there on, it's off to the races to eat and be merry. And remember, a nice large bowl of rice is key, just in case your mouth starts to catch on fire from Petra's spicy stir-fry.

Bon appétit, amigos.

tina basich: soup and

Tina Basich is the queen of snowboarding. Wait, that's not right, she's the crown princess of the hill. Ah, yes, that's more like it. How do I figure? Well, she's been doing it at the highest level for just about *ever*; she's got her own clothing line, and a signature board with Paul Frank graphics (and an animated short starring her and Paul Frank's characters), and is a graphic designer/artist in her own right; she was awarded the MTV Girls Who Kick Ass award; and she serves as faithful front woman for Boarding for Breast Cancer. Bottom line, Tina Basich might just be one of the greatest women of her time. Seriously.

Advice: Do what you like and like what you do

salad Dinner party

French Bread

Preheat oven to 350 degrees.
Cut French bread lengthwise and place on cookie sheet open
    sides up.
Butter bread and spread crushed garlic evenly.
Sprinkle on Parmesan cheese.
Cook until golden brown (7 to 12 minutes).

Soup

Preheat oven to 350 degrees.
Cut butternut squash in half and place facedown in a 9 x 12
    deep-dish baking pan.
Add 1 cup water and bake for 20 minutes
    or until tender.
On the stovetop in a large stockpot, mix 3 cans cream of aspara-
    gus soup, 3 cans creamed corn, and 1 can drained corn kernels
    over medium heat.
Shred cooked butternut squash with a fork and add to soup mix.
Stir in 2 tablespoons curry powder to taste and of course a dash
    of salt and pepper.

Salad

In a large bowl, pour 2 bags of mixed greens and add:
    1 chopped apple
    1 handful of diced walnuts
    1 handful of cranraisins
    1/3 cup crumbled blue cheese

Salad Dressing

1/4 cup olive oil
1/4 cup balsamic vinegar
2 tablespoons brown mustard and of course a dash of salt
    and pepper

Whisk with a fork and mix with the salad.

Bread

Butter

absolute no-no's

- **Don't butter the entire piece of bread in one spread.**

- **Never go back to the central communal butter source to butter your bread.**

- **DO NOT USE YOUR FORK OR SPOON TO BUTTER YOUR BREAD.**

- **Do not take more than one piece of bread from the basket per pass.**

G

J

C D

A. Dinner Plate
B. Salad Plate
C. Salad Fork
D. Dinner Fo
E. Dinner K
The Desser

etiquette 101 with Robert Earl

Bread 'n' Butter Basics, Baby

It's time to refine our social skills—to impress those in the know. This tip is a no-brainer, but at times it has plagued us all. "BREAD and BUTTER." Most of us can't wait to dive into the rolls. It's understandable: you've been starving all day and now you are a savage beast in need of some nourishment.

Here's What Happens
The bread basket rolls by. You need to take one and only one slice of bread or roll. No need to touch every piece for freshness either since other people aren't looking forward to your grimy fingers all over what they are about to consume. Place the chosen piece on your bread plate (which is on your upper left) and pass the rest on. Next is the butter issue. Listen carefully here. Do NOT butter the entire piece at once—this is very bad manners. You need to rip a small piece off, butter that, and then eat. Repeat steps for all future bites.

Bet You Didn't Know This
• Pass the bread before you stuff your face.

Some Rules of Thumb
• English muffins may be torn in half.
• Slices of bread, rolls, croissants, or muffins are torn into two or three bites at a time, buttered, then eaten before more is torn.

> Alright already, I know you really don't want to hear all these silly etiquette tips but I promise you if you just incorporate a few tactics you will be looking super sweet.
>
> Then when you have kids you'll pass it along. Bread and butter is a basic, you absolutely need to know it. When was the last time you didn't want to lay into that steamy loaf staring you in the eyes? Now you'll be able to go at it with grace and style.
>
> Read, eat, read, eat, surf, read, eat, snowride, and then to the skate park, with good manners, of course.

do they know? Which is the butter knife? Small or big?
(Random trivia only dorks know)

AARON MCGOVERN

"Well, I'm not really sure. We usually just have one knife at my house—it kinda does everything."

SWEET PUSSY FRANK

"Whoa, that's totally easy. The big one—then you can fit way more butter on it, right?"

SHAUN WHITE

"I never really noticed. I usually just eat my bread without butter."

MIKE "CARSACE" CARTER

"I strictly stick with my Mookie-Bear—it works just fine. Who needs butter anyway?"

Kahea Keikikanemuahanauiakalakonahea Hart has been surfing the globe for over twenty-three years. Despite surfing such spots as Tahiti, the Philippines, Mexico, Fiji, Bali, South Africa, Galapagos, Japan, Rarotonga, Peru, Chile, Western Australia, and Tasmania, nothing feels more like home for him than the North Shore of Oahu, where Backdoor is his front porch. But wait, there's more! There's even a witness to him airing into Mainline Pocket after six feet of fresh snow at Squaw Valley, CA. Kahea is the Hawaiian's Hawaiian. So when you see him in the lineup, you can say "what up," but don't try and drop in on him cuz you'll get a sock in the nose.

Kahea Hart: Egg White

Where'd it come from?
This recipe is what I eat for breakfast when I'm in training camp with Rob Garcia. I will also make this the morning of competition depending on what time my heat is.

BURRITOS

ingredients

3 pieces of garlic, onion, and mushrooms
1 tablespoon olive oil
4 to 5 eggs
Milk
Cheese (white, yellow, or moldy)
Leftover salad
Tortillas (corn or flour)
Salsa

what to do

Chop garlic, onion, and 'shrooms to the size you like, the smaller the better.
Heat small amount of olive oil in pan, at medium-high heat.
While the oil heats up, break open your eggs and separate them. Discard the yolks. Dump the egg whites in a bowl, add a small amount of milk, and beat with fork.
By now your oil is burning if you had a hard time with the eggs. Anyway, throw your garlic, onions, and 'shrooms in and fry until onions are almost clear. I listed leftover salad as an ingredient because I had removed the onions and tomatoes because they were already sliced.
Add the egg whites to your veggies, cook until your desired whiteness. Before you take the eggs off the heat, grate some cheese on them.
If you're on the low-fat plan, dump the eggs into a corn tortilla, but flour is fine.
Add salsa and roll the tortilla closed.

I hope you enjoy this breakfast—it will leave you full but not sleepy.
Aloha, Kahea

9

how to ollie

At the peak of your ollie, level out your board...

...then wait for the landing.

As you jump, your front foot slides up to the nose, pulling the board into the air.

Land with your knees bent. Keep your balance.

finish

With both your feet on the board, smack the tail to the ground with your back foot and jump off of that back foot—getting the timing down is probably the hardest part.

start

For more trick tip know-how check out willysantos.com

10

viva la with "Martha" ^ Robert Earl

chips and helmets

Chips and guacamole:

This is for those of you with absolutely no bowls. Yes, no bowls sounds a little weird, but I want to prepare you for any situation.

What you need: a helmet, a kneepad, and a few paper towels.

This is really easy. All you need to do is steady the helmet, line it with the paper towels, and then pour in the chips; the guacamole then simply goes into the kneepad—cover kneepad with paper towel and dump in the guac.

There you go. Viva la chips and dips.

You can't go wrong. Get the boys over, put on tanning lotion, and eat the chips pretending you're in Mexico bronzing and eating guac and chips. So sweet, so sweet.

Added bonus:

The salt from your sweat provides a nice tang to the chips and guac nestled in your protective gear. The paper towel filters out the moisture and salt crystals that form on the food side.

If you've mistakenly purchased unsalted chips, go out and do a bit of skating—the longer the sesh, the more salt buildup. And for that extra zing, try it without paper towels!

Where did my amigo?

What you need:
1. helmet 2. paper towels 3. chips 4. kneepad 5. guac

Take your pick: a Dave Mirra shoe by DC Shoes, Dave Mirra bike from Haro, Dave Mirra finger bike, Dave Mirra video game, Dave Mirra Trick Tips video, Dave Mirra cereal, Dave Mirra "Miracle Boy" bubble gum, or Dave Mirra's Super Tour. If there's something that twelve- to twenty-four-year-old guys are interested in, a sponsor will pay Dave Mirra to attach his name to it. And rightly so. All the way from his days

Dave Mirra:

with the Plywood Hoods to his status as the most decorated X Games competitor ever, Mirra has earned every bit of his fame and fortune.

His double backflip in San Francisco etched his place in extreme-sports history and Mirra continues to push for a triple or at the very least a few holes in one at one of the million or so golf courses near his home in North Carolina (oh yeah, he's an avid golfer).

Dave, one question. When was the last time you cooked it?
I cooked it for my girlfriend, Jennifer, on our first date. We've been together four years and she is still begging me to cook it again. I really miss that dinner. Let me warn you, if you're not looking for a serious girlfriend you might want to stick to something simple, like SpaghettiO's.

Good luck.

1/2 pound pork tenderloin
1/4 cup unsweetened pineapple juice
1/4 teaspoon ground ginger root
1/4 teaspoon red pepper sauce
1 clove garlic, finely chopped
Cooking spray
1 medium onion, chopped (1/2 cup)
1 small red bell pepper, cut into thin strips
2 tablespoons reduced-sodium soy sauce or fish sauce
3 cups cold cooked white rice
Chives, chopped for garnish
Soy sauce to your desired amount

Remove the fat from the pork. Cut the pork into 1/2-inch cubes.
Mix the pork, pineapple juice, ginger root, pepper sauce, and garlic in a glass or bowl. Cover and refrigerate about an hour before cooking.
Remove the pork from the marinade and drain. Spray a 12-inch skillet with no-stick cooking spray. Heat it over medium-high heat, add the pork, and stir-fry 5 to 10 minutes or until no longer pink. Remove the pork from the skillet.
Add the onion and bell pepper to the skillet; stir-fry about 8 minutes or until the onion is tender. Stir in the pork, soy sauce, and rice.
Cook about 10 minutes, stirring constantly, until the rice is hot and golden.
Sprinkle with chives; serve with soy sauce.

the mirra mix light

peter Line:

On **July 4, 1952,** a boy named Samuel McDanials was awarded a blue ribbon by Mayor Benjamin Rigor at the Broward County Fair in Broward County, Florida. It was a muggy 81 degrees. On July 12, 1952, at the Tallahassee County Cook-off, another blue ribbon was awarded to a boy named Samuel McDanials. The week following, in Miami, another blue ribbon was pinned to the shirt of Samuel McDanials. Samuel McDanials, only fifteen years old, brown scruffy hair and dirty fingernails, liked baseball and airplanes. He also had a secret recipe. Each of the blue ribbons awarded to Samuel McDanials during that humid summer were for his now-famous Tuna Noodle Casserole.

tuna noodle casserole

I don't know Samuel McDanials or his recipe. But here's mine:

ingredients

2 handfuls of noodles
    (any shape, size, color)
1 can of cream of mushroom soup
1 can of tuna in water
4 handfuls of potato chips

what to do

Cook noodles like you do spaghetti, and drain water.
Mix noodles, soup, and tuna in "casserole" plate thing. Crunch potato chips on top.
Either put it in the microwave for 2 to 10 minutes or in the oven at 350 degrees
    until potato chips are a golden brown.

The Florida state tree is the Sabal Palmetto Palm.

15

pots, pans & knives

Ok, ok, pots and pans are a must, so is a knife and a few other small tools, but what do you actually need? Probably a whole lot less than Williams Sonoma would tell you. Remember your mom's kitchen? There was probably a drawer full of tools that not only didn't get used, but also that nobody in the house knew what they were used for! So start simple and stick with the basics outlined below. Surprisingly, you can get this stuff cheap at garage sales or swap meets, but if your parents are taking you on a little kitchen-stocking shopping spree or if you happen to come upon some unexpected loot, buy the highest-quality items you can get. You're going to use this stuff every day and most quality kitchen tools will last a lifetime.

And don't forget, some of the recipes in this book might require a car's engine, a dishwasher, or even an iron. Like a busload of Boy Scouts, a good chef is always, always prepared.

Pots and Pans
What are you going to do? If you wanna cook, you've got to have a few pots and pans. Now, you can either steal these from your mum as you head out the door for college, have your girlfriend du jour buy you some, or actually plunk down your hard-earned money for them at a store. Remember, kids, a pot or a pan is likely to last you a lifetime or at least until you get married and your wife throws them all out, so make sure to buy the best you can possibly afford (All-Clad is my personal favorite).

If you don't have any money, don't be afraid; any old pot or pan that you can find at a local garage sale or thrift shop will do. The big old cast-iron babies are really great. So are wayward woks.

Basic Pots & Pans
10-inch skillet This is the pan that you are going to use the most. Look for one that is non-stick and don't be afraid to spend a couple of extra bucks on it—the more expensive the skillet, the better the cooking surface and the less likely it is to warp.

4-quart saucepan This is going to be good for medium jobs like heating up soup, spaghetti sauce, or just boiling some water.

8-quart pot Great for big jobs like cooking pasta and brewing up some homemade soup.

11 x 17-inch cookie sheet A must for heating up pizza, Bagel Bites, and of course slice-and-bake cookies.

4-quart saucepan

whoa.

10-inch skillet

Knives—Buy One, Make It Good!

What with their German names, expensive materials, and finely honed blades, knives can be one of the most costly things you'll need to buy for your kitchen. But don't despair, you can manage just about anything with just one—an all-purpose eight-inch chef's knife.

The culinary workhorse, a proper chef's knife has a wide blade that can manage anything you've got, from slicing and chopping to mincing and dicing. The blade has a slight, rounded curve to it so that you can use it to chop with a simple rocking motion. Even the broad, flat part of the blade is useful for crushing garlic. Buy the best one you can afford and make sure the metal goes all the way through the handle for the best possible buy, because you'll likely have it and use it for the rest of your live long days.

What other knives might you want to have on hand should you have a few extra bucks for stocking your kitchen? A three-inch paring knife for small jobs, like slicing an apple, or cutting the cheese, is a good companion to the bigger chef's knife. Also, having a long, serrated bread knife, a carving knife, and a meat cleaver around is always helpful but generally unnecessary. The further you stray from the basics, the less likely you'll be to use it.

butcher knife

Aaron McGovern:

This is my favorite dish. My mom made this for me growing up. She taught it to me when I went off to college. I knew I couldn't afford it in a restaurant and I couldn't go on without it. These days it's my favorite way to make chicken in an oven. This occurs mostly in the winter when it's too cold to barbeque and my lovely Annette wants to dine by the fire and watch some movies (or not watch some movies if I do a good job). This is also a good dish to make before a big day of crazy lines and big air.

It's a good source of carbohydrates to keep your carcass hucking all day long.

chicken parmesan

ingredients

Boneless chicken breasts, or a live
  chicken from Heckler's farm
Butter
Marinara sauce (plain is best)
2 eggs
Rosemary and thyme
Italian bread crumbs
Mozzarella cheese (cheddar can
  be substituted if it's all you got)

what to do

Wash the chicken and cover it with
  wax paper or Saran Wrap on a
  cutting board. Take a beer bottle
  and pound the chicken flat so it
  is uniformly thin.

Prepare a baking pan by greasing it with butter. This helps with taste and with cleanup. Dump in the marinara so
  that 1/4 inch coats the pan where you will place the chicken.

Break the eggs into a bowl with a little rosemary and thyme. In another bowl place the bread crumbs. Drop the
  chicken in the eggs, then the bread crumbs, and make sure all the chicken is covered. Brown the chicken in
  the frying pan. You're not cooking the chicken—just browning it. When done with that, place the chicken in
  the marinara in the pan.

Place more marinara on each piece of chicken. A nice coat tastes good. On top of the marinara spread grated
  mozzarella cheese. Spread the cheese like on a pizza. Once everything is in, bake the dish at 400 degrees for
  30 to 40 minutes or until the chicken is white all the way through.

I like to serve this dish with pasta, salad, garlic bread, and of course a nice red wine. It will fill you up so much
  you won't have to eat until late the next day, and the leftovers work great for sandwiches.

Good luck.

Etiquette 101 with Robert Earl

Table Basics

No matter where you are, basic rules apply:

1. When you're at the table with one or more people, you're not in bed scratching your ass, you're with people. So look them in the eyes, engage in conversation, and for Pete's sake, don't be a schmuck.

2. When you've been invited over to a friend's house for dinner, or even if you're just dropping by, bring a bouquet of flowers, a bottle of wine, a box of chocolates, or something else that shows you care. This will get you invited back for free meals again and again, thus saving you lots of money and gaining you lots of friends in the process. As in life, you've gotta give a little to get a little.

How to Eat: American vs. Continental Style

If you're an American and you were taught by your parents how to eat with utensils, you were told to hold your knife in your right hand and your fork in your left hand when cutting a bite to eat. Then, when you're going to raise that bite to your grille, you put the knife down on the edge of your plate, switch the fork to your right hand, and then chomp away. But, sit down to a meal with some Euros and you'll see that there's another way to eat. Call it the Continental or European style, this method of wielding your knife and fork is way more efficient and generally less formal than the North American way of eating.

Here's how it's done. Always keep the fork in your left hand and the knife in the right. Hold the food with the fork, cut with the knife, and, once a bit-size piece has been separated from the whole, put it directly into your mouth with the down-facing fork. This way, you don't put the knife down every time and transfer the fork to your right hand—as the North American tradition dictates.

> Sometimes rules change from country to country, or house to house. No ettiquette is set in stone. So, remember a few basics. Don't be a schmuck, always smile, say please and thank you, and as Terje says, "Never wear your hat at the table." The rest is up to you.

(Random trivia only dorks know)

do they know? How do American and European dining styles differ?

ALIBABA

"I'm American, so I eat like a European, and vice versa. I think, wait..."

TINA BASICH

"I've been to Europe, and I think they are a lot more casual over there. You can chew loudly."

HECKLER

"German beer is way better than American beer."

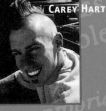
CAREY HART

"It depends on which arm is in a cast."

20

FOOD **for thought**

with *Robert Earl*

+

+

=

Well, this is an easy one.

What could possibly go better with blue bubble gum soda than vanilla ice cream? It's almost like the bubble gum flavor at Baskin-Robbins without the gum balls.

1st - you want to get a blender, any sort will do.

2nd - pure vanilla ice cream (Breyers is the best).

3rd - put 4 heaping scoops in blender.

4th - pour one 12 oz bottle of Jones blue bubble gum soda in the blender.

5th - Blend.

Now pour, one for you, one for a friend, whip cream and a cherry, and hold on...

It will definitely knock your socks off.

X 21

cooking terms

Robert Earl

a

A la carte: Something on a menu that is sold all by itself (i.e., it doesn't come with fries and a Coke).

Al dente: From an Italian saying that means "to the tooth," this is when something is cooked to the point where it's just starting to turn soft, but is still very firm (ah...firm...).

b

Baking powder: The white stuff that makes bread and cakes rise because it releases CO_2 bubbles from whatever it is put into.

Baking soda: This white stuff is actually contained in baking powder—it makes things fizz.

Baste: To consistently lube up something that you're cooking with a coat of liquid-like sauce, marinade, melted butter, meat drippings, or some kind of stock.

Beat: If you're a guy and you're over about twelve years old, you don't need a definition for this one. A good rule of thumb is that 100 strokes by hand is equal to about one minute of abuse with an electric mixer.

Blanch: Take a pot of boiling water, drop something like a tomato into it very briefly, pull it out, and dunk it into freezing cold water. You've just blanched something.

Blend: Mix two or more things together. If you didn't already know this, please put this book down and return to first grade.

Broil: To cook the living hell out of something in a hurry, the broiler is usually under the main compartment of your oven.

c

Casserole: Something that your aunt makes because it's cheap and easy. Technically a casserole is both a type of food and the pan that such a food is cooked in. Confused? Then just stay away from this stuff.

Chop: To whack the hell out of something with quick blows from a knife or cleaver. Also a cut of meat taken from the rib section of an animal that includes part of the rib.

Crêpe: Don't let anyone kid you, this is just the French word for "pancake."

d

Dash: A measuring term referring to a very small amount of seasoning added to food with a quick, downward stroke of the hand. In general, a dash can be considered to be somewhere between a scant 1/16 and 1/8 teaspoon.

Devein: To remove the gray-black vein from the back of a shrimp.

Dice: To cut food into tiny (about 1/8- to 1/4-inch) cubes.

Dissolve: To incorporate a dry ingredient (such as sugar, salt, yeast, or gelatin) into a liquid.

Dredge: To lightly coat food to be fried, as with eggs, flour, cornmeal, or bread crumbs. This coating helps brown the food.

Dutch oven: Eat large quantities of garlic. Lie in bed. Snuggle with mate under covers. Silently flatulate and lock covers tightly so that bed partner cannot escape.

f

Fermentation: A process by which food goes through a chemical change. Fermentation alters the appearance and/or flavor of foods and beverages such as beer, buttermilk, cheese, wine, vinegar, and yogurt. Leave some apple juice in your closet for a few months and taste. You'll see what we mean.

Fillet: A strip or compact piece of boneless meat or fish.

Flambé: French for "flamed" or "flaming," this method of food presentation consists of sprinkling certain foods with liquor, which, after warming, is ignited just before serving.

g

Garnish: A decorative, edible accompaniment to finished dishes, from appetizers to desserts. Garnishes can be placed under, around, or on food, depending on the dish.

Gelatin: An odorless, tasteless, and colorless thickening agent, which when dissolved in hot water and then cooled forms a jelly.

Giblets: Generally, the term "giblets" refers to the heart, liver, and gizzard of domesticated fowl and game birds.

Gratin: A dish that is topped with cheese or bread crumbs mixed with bits of butter, then heated in the oven or under the broiler until brown and crispy.

h

Haggis: This Scottish specialty is made by stuffing a sheep's (or other animal's) stomach lining with a minced mixture of the animal's organs (heart, liver, lungs, and so on), onion, suet, oatmeal, and seasonings, then simmering the sausage in water for about 4 hours.

Hops: A hardy, vine-type plant that produces conelike flowers. The dried flowers are used to impart a pleasantly bitter flavor to beers and ales.

Hummus: This thick Middle Eastern spread is made from mashed chickpeas seasoned with lemon juice, garlic, and olive or sesame oil. It's usually served as a dip with pieces of pita, or as a sauce.

j

Jell: To congeal a food substance, often with the aid of gelatin.

k

Kabob or Kebab: Small chunks of meat, fish, or shellfish that are usually marinated before being threaded on a skewer and grilled over coals.

Kirsch: From the German *kirsche* ("cherry") and *wasser* ("water"), this clear brandy is distilled from cherry juice and pits.

Knead: To mix and work into a uniform mass, as by folding, pressing, and stretching with the hands.

Kosher: To prepare in conformity with the requirements of the Jewish dietary law.

l

Lactose: This sugar occurs naturally in milk and is also called milk sugar.

Lager: Beer that is stored in its cask or vat until free of sediment and crystal clear. It's a light, bubbly, golden brew that ranks as America's most popular.

Leavener: Agents that are used to lighten the texture and increase the volume of baked goods such as breads, cakes, and cookies.

Loin: Get your head out of the gutter, we're talking food now. Depending on the animal, the loin comes from the area on both sides of the backbone extending from the shoulder to the leg (for pork) or from the rib to the leg (in beef, lamb, and veal). Like your tenderloin, get it?

m

Malt: Grain, usually barley, that has been allowed to sprout, used chiefly in brewing and distilling an alcoholic beverage, such as beer or ale.

Marinate: To soak a food such as meat, fish, or vegetables in a seasoned liquid mixture.

Mince: To cut food into very small pieces. Minced food is in smaller pieces than chopped food.

Mousse: A French term meaning "froth" or "foam," mousse is a rich, airy dish that can be sweet or savory, hot or cold.

p

Pinch: A measuring term referring to the amount of a dry ingredient (such as salt or pepper) that can be held between the tips of the thumb and forefinger. It's equivalent to approximately 1/16 teaspoon.

Poach: To cook food gently in liquid just below the boiling point.

Proof: A term used to indicate the amount of alcohol in liquor or other spirits. To dissolve yeast in a warm liquid (sometimes with a small amount of sugar) and set it aside in a warm place for 5 to 10 minutes until it swells and becomes bubbly. This technique proves that the yeast is alive and active and therefore capable of leavening a bread or other baked good.

Puree: Any food that is finely mashed to a smooth, thick consistency.

r

Render: To melt animal fat over low heat so that it separates from any connective pieces of tissue.

Roux: A mixture of flour and fat that, after being slowly cooked over low heat, is used to thicken mixtures such as soups and sauces.

s

Sauté: To fry lightly in butter or fat in a shallow open pan.

Scald: To heat a liquid (such as milk) almost to the boiling point.

Score: To make shallow cuts (usually in a diamond pattern) in the surface of certain foods such as meat or fish. This is done for several reasons: as a decoration on some foods (breads and meats), as a means of assisting flavor absorption (as with marinated foods), to tenderize less tender cuts of meat, and to allow excess fat to drain during cooking.

Sear: To brown meat quickly by subjecting it to very high heat either in a skillet, under a broiler, or in a very hot oven.

Shred: To cut food into narrow strips, either by hand or by using a grater or a food processor fitted with a shredding disk.

Sift: To put (flour, for example) through a sieve or other straining device in order to separate the fine from the coarse particles.

Simmer: To cook food gently in liquid at a temperature (about 185°F) low enough that tiny bubbles just begin to break the surface.

Slow Cooker (Crock-Pot): An electric "casserole" that cooks food with low, steady, moist heat. It's designed to cook food over a period of 8 to 12 hours.

Steam: A method of cooking whereby food is placed on a rack or in a special steamer basket over boiling or simmering water in a covered pan.

Stir-fry: To quickly fry small pieces of food in a large pan over very high heat while constantly and briskly stirring the food.

Stout: A strong, dark beer that originated in the British Isles. Stout is more redolent of hops than regular beer and is made with dark-roasted barley, which gives it a deep, dark color and bittersweet flavor.

Suet: Found in beef, sheep, and other animals, suet is the solid white fat found around the kidneys and loins.

t

Tart: A pastry crust with shallow sides, containing pastry, jelly, or fruit.

Truffle: Various fleshy, ascomycetous, edible fungi that grow underground on or near the roots of trees and are valued as a delicacy that only pigs can sniff out. Truffles also are chocolate confections, especially one made of a mixture including chopped nuts, rolled into balls and covered with cocoa powder.

Tureen: A broad, deep, usually covered dish used for serving foods such as soups or stews.

v

Vegan: A vegetarian who eats plant products only (and no butter, cheese, eggs, and milk), especially one who uses no products derived from animals (as fur or leather).

Vegetarian: One who eats no meat or fish or (often) any animal products.

w

Whip: A gelatin-based dessert that's airy and light because of the addition of either whipped cream or stiffly beaten egg whites. Beating ingredients makes air flow through them, which increases their volume until they are light and fluffy.

Whisk: A kitchen utensil consisting of a series of looped wires forming a three-dimensional teardrop shape. The wires are joined and held together with a long handle. Whisks are used for whipping ingredients.

Wine: Naturally fermented juice of grapes. More broadly, the term can include alcoholic beverages created from other fruits and even vegetables (see fermentation).

y

Yeast: The sediments you see at the bottom of fruit juices that cause fermentation. It's fungi that tastes nasty by itself but makes bread rise and gives beer that buzz.

z

Zest: The perfumy outermost skin layer of citrus fruit (usually oranges or lemons), which is removed with the aid of a citrus zester, paring knife, or vegetable peeler. Only the colored portion of the skin (and not the white pith) is considered the zest.

In the country of Tibet, it's good manners to stick your tongue out at your guests.

how to wax a snowboard

Alright, a little break from the food. So you need to get out on the mountain and you haven't eaten for days. Well, here it is: kill two birds with one stone—wax your board and scramble some eggs.

Waxing Your Snowboard

WHAT YOU'LL NEED:
Some things you will absolutely need, others are optional (the vises are really sweet, especially for cooking, but they aren't mandatory).

The Wax: Be sure to buy ski or snowboard wax that is designed to be applied with a hot iron. There are plenty of choices, but a good all-temperature wax will work well in most snow conditions.

The Scraper: Pick this up at your favorite board shop along with the wax. Plastic or metal scrapers are both fine, just avoid really wide scrapers that are sometimes marketed "just for" snowboards—they suck.

The Iron: Although they do make specialty ones with smooth bottoms, any type will do (i.e., the one you stole from your mum will be just fine).

The Scotchbrite: These rough green pads are available at any grocery store next to the kitchen sponges. Pick a few up, you'll need one for your dishes anyway.

OPTIONAL BUT HELPFUL ITEMS:

Base Cleaner: If your snowboard's base is dirty, clean it using a base cleaner (find this at your board shop) and a rag before you hot wax it.

Vises: Setting up a workbench makes tuning and waxing your board much easier. You can buy small vises that will hold your snowboard in place while you work.

Let's Get Started

1. Drip
Put an old sheet or some newspaper on the floor to catch dripping wax. Then put your board base up on your new vises or on some books.

Plug in your iron and set it to a medium heat. It should be hot enough to readily melt the wax, but not so hot that the wax smokes. Hold the iron lengthwise, press the wax bar against the hot iron, and hold it there. As the wax drips, move the iron up and down the base of your board until you have drips all over the place.

2. Iron
Now iron in all that wax until the base of your board is fully covered. Keep the iron moving. Whatever you do, don't stop moving the iron!

3. Scrape
Wait about fifteen minutes for the wax to set and cool. Now grab the scraper and scrape off any excess wax, working from the nose to the tail. Scraping away all the wax may sound counterproductive, until you realize that hot wax actually opens up the pores in a snowboard's base—and stays in the place you want the wax to go.

4. Buff
After scraping, rub the Scotchbrite pad in a nose-to-tail motion to take off the last of the wax and give your board a super sweet finish.

cooking with an iron

Ok, you've just finished waxing the board and the iron is still hot (this is where the saying "strike when the iron's still hot" comes from).

I would have to say at times it's totally cool to do some alternative cooking; it helps mix things up a bit.

First, you're going to need to get some

aluminum foil. Crimp it into a bowl of sorts. This is fairly easy, just check the photos here.

Now that your foil pan is ready to go, grab an egg or two and crack away. Now use a knife or a screwdriver and scramble those babies.

Next you're ready to balance the iron in

one hand and heat the eggs by setting your foil on top. In about 4 to 6 minutes breakfast is served.

Feel free to drop some toast right in there or actually lay it on the workbench and iron the shiaaat out of it all. Aaaaah, eggs 'n' toast.

Boom! Breakfast is served.

Additional Iron Uses

Grilled cheese

Boiled water (be very patient)

Reheat pizza

Sausages

In the Kitchen with Robert Earl

microwave hints

Refresh stale potato chips in the microwave. Just place a plateful in for about 30 to 45 seconds, then let stand for 1 minute. The guests will never know you've had these babies lying around for weeks.

Toast coconut in the microwave. Watch coconut closely, stir every 30 seconds for 2 minutes and keep it in for a total of 4 minutes.

Rock-hard ice cream will take about a minute and 30 seconds, then it's ready for action.

Try the old microwave cheese. So good. White bread and a slice of cheese—30 seconds will do.

Soften hard brown sugar. Go ahead put it in with a cup of water sitting next to it. Before you know it, it's smooth as silk.

Soften butter for 30 seconds at about 50 percent for that perfect buttery effect.

For the stamp collectors out there. Place a couple drops of water on the stamp to be removed. Put it in the nuker for 20 seconds and the stamp will come right off.

Thaw frozen orange juice right in its container. 30 to 45 seconds should do, then just add to a pitcher of water.

Burritos from 7-Eleven do quite well in the microwave.

Do not put in pets or any other creature you might stumble across. This is called sociopathic behavior and is considered quite uncool and very illegal.

Drying ski gloves and socks works but is not recommended.

kitchen emergency

food hits the floor

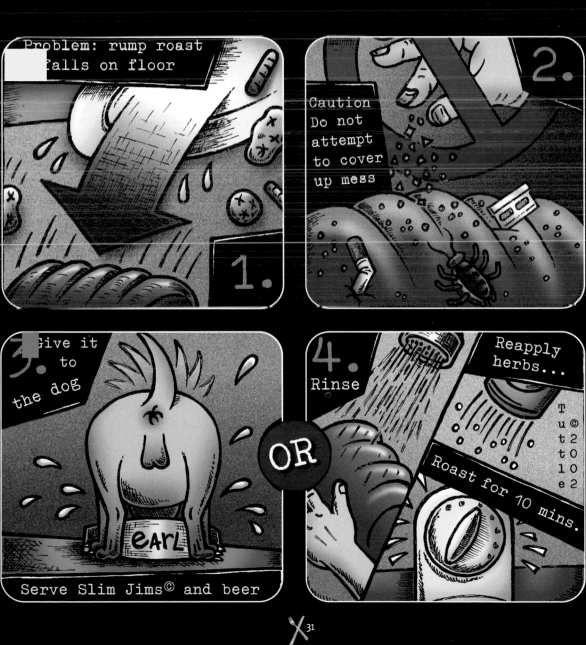

Problem: rump roast falls on floor

1.

Caution Do not attempt to cover up mess

2.

3. Give it to the dog

the dog

OR

4. Rinse

Reapply herbs...

© Tuttle 2002

Roast for 10 mins.

EARL

Serve Slim Jims© and beer

X 31

Danny Way: Shark

ingredients

1/2 cup slivered almonds
2 tablespoons butter
2 tablespoons chopped parsley
6 tablespoons melted butter
1 tablespoon grated lemon rind
2 tablespoons freshly squeezed lemon juice
4 shark fillets (Swordfish or mahimahi may
    be substituted if shark is unavailable.)
4 tablespoons sherry
1 pinch freshly ground pepper
1/2 pound bacon; fried and crumbled
4 green onions, chopped
Lemon wedges

what to do

Lightly brown the almonds in the butter and
    set aside. Add parsley, butter, lemon rind,
    and juice.
Rub both sides of the fillets with the sherry
    and place on a broiler pan. Sprinkle with
    pepper.
Spoon some of the butter mixture over each
    fillet. Broil for 5 to 10 minutes, depending
    on the thickness of the fillets.
Turn over, spoon on more butter sauce, and
    continue broiling until done. Do not
    overcook or the fish will be dry.
Remove to a serving platter.
Sprinkle with the almonds, bacon, and green
    onions. Garnish with lemon wedges.

Serves two people.

alien workshop
LIFE FORCE

amandine

Danny Way lives a fairly quiet life. Besides almost breaking his neck literally and jumping out of a helicopter, he spends time cooking, being a father, fishing from his boat, and, no joke, growing palm trees .

The helicopter—oh, that happened when Danny built a twenty-foot-high vert ramp to attempt the world record of highest air (16.5 feet) and while breaking this record he, just for kicks, decided to jump out of a helicopter and land on the ramp. He pulled it off as he does with just about everything he tries, a true pioneer in the skate world, from street in the good old days to vert right here and now. This is all on top of being one of the most influential and progressive skaters of the twenty-first century.

Danny shares a little something from the California coast. It has to do with sharks, and no, he's not scared of them at all.

Brad Holmes

shane dorian:

The Big Island God of Style! Somehow Shane-O manages to pull it all down from his jungle hideaway on the Big Island—including getting married to his longtime lady in December 2001 and finding time to paint.

What does this master of style eat when he's not grubbin' his favorite beef teriyaki at the Kona Mixed Plate? ("They know my order cuz I eat there almost every single day.") What kinda Jungle Surprise does Dorian have in store? None other than the most popular dish to come out of the fiftieth state—poke.

What the hell is this? I hope it's better than a "poke" in the eye.

Well, poke (pronounced poe-kay) is perhaps the most celebrated of all traditional Hawaiian food. It's simple to make and it tastes incredible.

Do you remember when you first made this stuff?
I first made it for myself, at home in Kona, Hawaii, when I was barely out of high school. I remember not having a recipe and just kind of guessing at the ingredients.

How about before a competition?
I always try to eat clean, natural foods. Generally lots of fish, and lots of veggies!

X-iquette

Absolutely always eat poke with chopsticks—it just won't taste the same with a fork.

real Hawaiian ahi poke

ingredients

1 pound ahi (yellowfin tuna) cut into 1-inch cubes
4 teaspoons soy sauce
1 cup chopped onion
4 teaspoons chopped green onion
3 teaspoons sesame oil
1 teaspoon sesame seeds
1/4 cup Nori Furikake Japanese seasoning (optional)

what to do

Place ahi cubes in a mixing bowl, add all other
    ingredients, and mix well.
Serve chilled.
Enjoy with chopsticks.

Mike "Carsace" Carter has been seen on E! channel's *WILD ON* series as well as host of the now-defunct Bluetorch action-sports television series. He's also the cofounder of Electric eyewear, the company that sponsors athletes like Colin McKay, Bam Margera, Peter Line, Ozzie Wright, and Luke Egan.

One of the world's greatest bachelors, some say he's the real-life International Man of Mystery, whose antics around the industry, and 24/7 lifestyle, are legendary.

Why It Works/The Theory:
The theory behind this recipe is the fact that honey is a very seductive ingredient, and if utilized in the right capacity can be a sensual and inspiring treat for some late-night fun. An innocent and unsuspecting snack, it's also a tasty icebreaker.

Etiquette Tip:
Be aggressive when eating! Laugh about it, go for it, and MOST importantly you MUST lick the excess honey off your significant other's fingers whenever and wherever possible. THIS IS THE GOLDEN RULE. It is considered poor etiquette to JUST lick off your own fingers. This is key to the success of this recipe!

Who I Served This to the First Time:
Well, we'll just have to give her the code name of "Sharisa" and leave it at that.

My super secret seduction recipe is now public knowledge, so you bachelors owe me one...

ingredients

1 envelope microwave popcorn (I prefer Pop-time)
1 can chocolate powder
1 bottle of syrup (Aunt Jemima, of course!)
1 bottle of honey in a plastic "Honey Bear" squeeze bottle. ABSOLUTELY NO SUBSTITUTIONS ON THIS INGREDIENT!
1 big old bowl

what to do

Pop the corn in a microwave oven, being careful NOT to burn it. Overcook the corn and you are DONE from the start.

Next, pour the corn into the largest bowl you can find—it can't be too big.

Then, sprinkle on the chocolate powder generously.

You're going good. Now, douse the whole thing with syrup.

Now the crucial step: grab the "HONEY BEAR" bottle, but don't pour it on just yet! No premature pouring of the honey.

Here's the big move: you walk into the living room where your date is sitting on the couch waiting. You present the bowl of popcorn to your date and in her full view, proceed to pour the honey out of the "Honey Bear" and onto the warm popcorn!

Yes! When your date inquires about the bear say, "It's my little Mookie-Bear!" A warm and positive response should follow. Maybe several warm and positive responses if you've been a really good boy.

You'll want to serve with a glass of Merlot, poured in a champagne flute if available for that classy touch of, ya know!!

MOOKIE-BEAR POPCORN

**The Inspiration
(in his own words):**
This is a little recipe inspired by my need to have a "program" for when I invite a date over to my house for a movie, snack, wine, and some chillin'. Because if you really want things to go right with your date, you gotta have a bit of "flare and flava" for your nibbles!

My friends and I have always used the code word "Mookie-Bear," meaning a really cute girl that we'd like to hang out with. The correlation between the "Honey Bear" ingredient and your lady friend "Mookie-Bear" is a classic mix for this tantalizing and seductive recipe.

X-iquette

I'm a firm believer that it's never proper etiquette to "kiss and tell."

Jimbo morgan: medit

Don't smack your lips at the dinner table. Eat with your mouth closed.
The sound of someone smacking his lips is disturbing.

A Lake Tahoe fixture for almost two decades, Jimbo has pleasured himself in more ways than one, including skiing, snowboarding, and telemarking.
"King of The Hill" ruler for years, and let's not forget the Olympics. Yes, the Olympics. Speed skiing, that is. Make sure to ask Jimbo to see the Olympic rings tattooed on his back.

Who did you first make it for and where?
I made it for my girlfriend at her house when we got back from Greece.

What is your favorite food?
Hands down it's got to be SUSHI.

Do you eat anything before you go out to ski or snowboard?
I always have at least a latte and maybe a protein bar of some sort.

How many times do you cook or eat out?
Right now I'm just finishing building my house so I've been eating out quite a bit. But once my kitchen is done I hope I get to stay home and use all the recipes in this sweet book.

erranean Risotto

ingredients

4 3/4 cups chicken broth
4 cloves garlic, finely chopped
1 1/2 cups uncooked arborio or other short-grain white rice
2 cups broccoli flowerets
3/4 cup crumbled Feta cheese
1/2 cup oil-packed sun-dried tomatoes, drained and chopped
1 teaspoon dried oregano leaves
1 can (2 1/4 ounces) sliced ripe olives, drained

what to do

Heat 1/4 cup of the broth and the garlic to boiling in a 12-inch nonstick skillet over medium-high heat. Stir in the rice. Cook 1 minute, stirring constantly.

Pour 1/2 cup of the broth over the rice mixture. Cook uncovered over medium heat, stirring occasionally, until the liquid is absorbed.

Continue cooking 15 to 20 minutes, adding the broth 1/2 cup at a time and stirring occasionally, until the rice is creamy and almost tender.

Stir in the remaining ingredients. Cook just a couple more minutes and WAH-LAH. Mediterranean Risotto.

When you learn how to skate at America's most competitive park—the Encinitas, California, YMCA—when you're just six years old, when you've got a fully stamped passport before you've got a driver's license, and when you've got a legend like Hawk singing your praises, chances are you've got a bright future in the world of action sports.

Yet, Shaun White has shown that the future is *now* with his astounding win in the 2001 edition of the Arctic Challenge, where he was judged by a jury of the best riders in the world. He was the hottest rider on the biggest terrain available. It doesn't get much better than that—except for workin' with Tony Hawk, which White has done with frightening regularity.

shaun white: italian

Whether he's skating or snowboarding, you'll hear the crowd chanting "Future Boy" when White's on the scene, but the truth is that right now *is* Future Boy's time.

ingredients

1 stick margarine
1 cup vegetable oil
2 cups sugar
4 eggs
2 tablespoons anise seeds
4 teaspoons baking powder
1 16-ounce package of sliced almonds
4 cups flour

what to do

Beat the first three ingredients together for 10 minutes. Then add the eggs and mix for 5 minutes on medium speed.

Then mix the anise seeds, baking powder, and almonds into a fine texture in the blender. Add the egg mixture and beat for 5 minutes. Add 2 cups flour, blend, then add 2 more cups flour. If the dough seems sticky add more flour by hand while kneading dough on a floured board (so it doesn't stick).

Divide the dough into four pieces, roll it out by hand and make the dough the length of a cookie sheet and as wide as your hand (approximately 1 inch thick).

Preheat the oven to 350 degrees and bake for 30 minutes until light brown. Slice into 1-inch thick slices with a sharp knife and put the slices back in the oven for 8 more minutes .

You can add cranberries and macadamia nuts, chocolate chips, raisins, even peanut butter—**just don't use the anise seeds.**

cookies

Where did it come from?
This is what we make at Christmastime. My great-grandmother gave me the recipe.

What's your favorite food?
Sushi. But I also love Mac 'n' Cheese, Cup-a-Soup, and Rice Krispy treats with peanut butter.

Do you eat anything special before an event or demo?
Yes. Pear Luc (not sure how to spell his name but he's a vert skater)—he told me if I eat a bloody rare steak before events I will land all my tricks. So now, before the finals, I always go to Chart House and get a sirloin steak and a mud pie.

viva la "Martha" with Robert Earl

totally tubular place settings

So you are having a dinner party and you wanna make it all big and fancy? That means you'll need place settings, so here's an exciting way to make it happen for a great-smelling table that gives your guests that little something extra.

Added bonus:
All waxes smell different. Some smell like rootbeer, others are tropical, flower-scented, or just plain nasty. Pick the proper scent for each occasion. Rootbeer could be for the more informal gathering, whereas tropical could work at an impromptu bachelor party!

First thing: purchase some wax at your local surf shop. Any kind will do. I always search for Air Wax, but classic Mr. Zogs Sex Wax is always good. You'll also need a quarter and/or a paperclip. Take the quarter and carve a groove in the wax, then insert the paper clip and put your name card right there. Done.

A business gathering? Place a business card in the paper clip. More casual? Have an artist come in and draw a picture of each person, or a funky rendition of their name. Also, remember to set the table boy, girl, boy, girl, boy, girl—to mix it all up.

That's it—instant place settings, for little money and a whole lotta wax that your guests can take home and use for their morning sessions.

Total party network!

What you need:

1. surfboard wax
2. quarter and paper clip
3. paper or business card

44

Does Your Pee Smell Bad?

What foods make your urine smell especially bad? If you've ever had even the tiniest bit of asparagus you know what we're talking about. A big plate of broccoli can do it too, and so can cabbage and just about any other vegetable in high quantity. Spicy foods make your urine more pungent and some people claim that milk can change the smell of your pee.

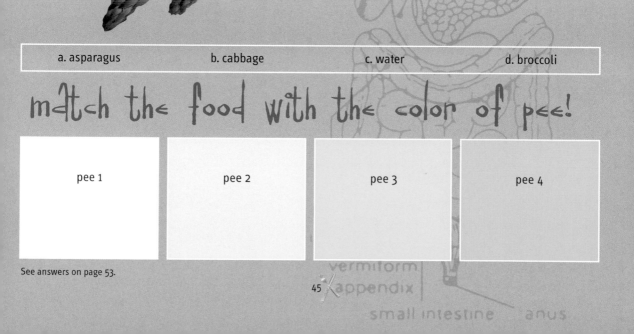

| a. asparagus | b. cabbage | c. water | d. broccoli |

match the food with the color of pee!

| pee 1 | pee 2 | pee 3 | pee 4 |

See answers on page 53.

miKe "rooftop" escamilla:

The recipe origin: I had asked my mom what goes in salsa and I just started to experiment after that until I came up with this recipe. Of course I never measure so all these measurements are made up—good luck.

I first made it while living in Big Bear years ago with my buddy Jason Mertz. We used to take turns making salsa. We would make huge bowls and eat it on everything—fish, omelettes, steak, whatever we were eating. He would always brag how much better his salsa was over mine, but look whose salsa made it into the cookbook...

—What's up now, Jason?

Mexican food is my favorite food—uh, wait , I mean

my wife's cooking.

That's it—that's what I'm supposed to say, right? I want to be honest but it's not worth a week
on the couch.

salsa fa nu

ingredients

2 tablespoons diced white onion
8 Roma tomatoes
2 to 3 tablespoons cilantro, chopped
2 diced jalapeños (no seeds)
2 serrano chiles, diced
1 teaspoon salt (add more if needed)
1 tablespoon lime juice (either from concentrate or
    just squeeze a slice in)

what to do

After you've chopped everything up, put it all in a mixing bowl and blend the
ingredients. Try the salsa with a chip and see if you have to add more of
ingredients that don't stand out enough.

Cover and refrigerate for a couple of hours. The longer it sits,
the more the flavors will blend. I hope it's good; if not,
blame Robert Earl—he made me do this!!

Now go jump off a building (see page 61).

He's the Wilt Chamberlain to Tony Hawk's Michael Jordan. He was the first skater to ever have a signature shoe (the legendary Vans CAB and Half Cab), he was the head of a punk band before punk was ever cool. CAB has been at the core of skating for over twenty years and doesn't show any signs of slowing down.

steve caballero :

Where did it come from?
Well...I had a roommate back in the day who is still actually a great friend of mine, John Pecoraro (who is a great cook, by the way). We would take turns making salsa. He'd have his secret ingredients and I'd have mine, so it was a battle of who could make the best salsa. Well, it turns out that the more we tried to outdo each other, the better both of our salsas tasted! I credit my buddy John for the ingredients, which I adapted to my own recipe.

Do you eat anything special before an event or demo?
I used to eat pasta before competitions because my old team manager, Stacy Peralta, would say that the carbs would help me out the next day for strength and endurance. I did it for a few years, but now I'll eat pretty much anything that sounds or looks good!

X-iquette

Well, make sure your guests are salsa connoisseurs and if they like it hot, make it hot, but be aware that you may have to tone it down a little for some.

How many times a week do you cook or eat out?
I only cook if I have my daughter Kayla around, but I pretty much eat out all the time. There are too many great restaurants around my spot in San Jose, California.

super salsa

ingredients

4 large red tomatoes
1 red bell pepper
1 green bell pepper
3 small serrano peppers
2 small jalapeño peppers
1 bundle cilantro
1 large white onion
1 small lime or lemon
1 sprinkle of sugar
1 teaspoon salt
1 sprinkle of ground pepper

My least favorite food would be cheese and anything that can't be made without it!

what to do

Grab a large bowl, a sharp knife, and a cutting board. Dice up the tomatoes.

Chop both bell peppers and place them in the bowl.

Slice up the serrano peppers as fine as you can get them; same goes for the jalapeño peppers.

Cut the stems off the cilantro and chop up the leaves as fine as possible. Don't use too much and be sure to only use a nice handful. Add it to the hot peppers and mix them together.

Grab the onion last (since for some reason it makes you have watery eyes) and dice it up. Place that in the bowl and mix again.

Cut the lime or lemon in half and squeeze the juice from both halves into the salsa.

Add the sugar, salt, and ground pepper and mix thoroughly.

Place in the fridge and chill for half an hour and then take it out.

Open up a bag of Tostitos chips and dig in. Beware... once you start, you won't be able to stop eating until the whole bowl is finished. Enjoy!

Don't forget the chips. I recommend the Tostitos brand 100% White Corn Restaurant Style!

sergie ventura

Where'd the recipe come from?

It's just some special technique my mother has been doing for years and I believe she got it from my grandmother.

Who did you first make it for and where?

I made it for myself when I was sixteen. Officially, I was watching my mom set it up and I asked her if I could do the rest, but I still had a hand in it.

What's your favorite food?

I like a variety of foods. Traveling so much has given me eclectic tastes. I have to say, though, that I really can't turn down a good ol' homecooked meal. I have come to enjoy Japanese, Italian, and an English "fry-up." I also love home-baked goods like cookies, cupcakes, and brownies. I've got a little bit of a sweet tooth, you see.

Do you eat anything special before an event or demo?

Actually, I like to eat carbohydrates and protein before a long day of skating. I try to drink plenty of fluids as well. Things like pasta, breads, and most important, vegetables. I never used to like them when I was a kid, but I grew into liking them more and more as I got older. For protein, I like to eat red meat or some kind of chicken dish.

How many times a week do you cook or eat out?

Most of the time I'm on the road so I really don't have a choice but to go out and eat. That's why I can never turn down a home-cooked meal. I have so much appreciation for it and for those who prepare it.

X-iquette

Always be a gentleman. It's easy to act that way, but can you be that way naturally and consistently?

ingredients

2 cups cooking oil
1 egg
1 cup regular flour
1 teaspoon salt
1 teaspoon pepper
1 teaspoon Accent seasoning
1 teaspoon garlic powder
2 center cut pork chops

what to do

Preheat the stove to a medium heat and pour the 2 cups
   of oil in the frying pan. Then beat the egg in a bowl
   big enough for the pork chop to fit down into.
On a separate plate, mix the cup of flour, the salt,
   and the pepper. Put the flour plate right next to
   the frying pan with the egg beaten in a bowl
   next to that, making an assembly line.
Then grab your pork chops and season them
   on both sides with salt, pepper, Accent
   (or some other all-purpose seasoning),
   and a few shakes of garlic powder.
Ok, you're ready to cook. Start by dipping
   the meat into the beaten egg and
   then placing it onto the plate with
   the flour. Make sure that you completely
   cover both sides of each chop with flour.
   Then drop the chops into the frying pan and
   cook each side on medium heat for at least
   15 minutes, until it's golden brown.
Then, the secret to this recipe, you lower the heat to
   medium-low and continue to cook the chops for 20
   minutes on each side with a lid on the pan. When you're
   done cooking them, pull the chops from the oil and
   drop them on a plate covered with paper towels
   to absorb the grease. You should have a super
   tender inside with a light crispy shell that
   will seriously melt in your mouth.

how to fix a flat

Stop Riding
You can't fix a flat tire while you're in motion.

Start Fixing
Either take the bike to a bike shop and let them deal with it or start fixing the thing by letting all the air out of the tube.

Bust Off the Wheel
It's easy. Turn your bike upside down and remove the axle nuts with a 15mm box wrench or a crescent wrench (the bigger the better). You may have to release your brakes to get the wheel to move through the brake pads.

If you have a really slow leak it is possible to patch the tube without taking the wheel off, but that's a royal-pain-in-the-arse way to do it and should only be attempted by the laziest and stupidest among you.

Bust Off the Tire
So, you've got the wheel off, now pull the tire off the wheel. On most BMX bikes the tires are loose enough that you might be able to pull it off with your bare hands. Start by pulling one side up and over the edge of the rim. Once you have a good portion of one side off the whole thing will get easier and your wheel and tire will soon be two. Once the tire is off, pull the tube out of it.

Patch or Replace
It's always better to replace a tube than to patch one, and if you have a big blowout, patching probably won't be an option. Still, for those who are extra low on funds patching is worth a try. Most bike shops have small glueless patches that just stick on a small hole like a Band-Aid, so it's pretty easy.

Figure Out What Caused the Flat
Whatever garbage caused your flat is probably still sticking in your tire, so you'll want to check that out. Pull the tire completely off the rim and run your hand carefully on the inside of it, feeling for glass or other sharp objects, and also inspecting the tire to make sure there's not a large cut or hole in it. Also give your rim a check and make sure that there aren't any spokes sticking through the rim strip. That can cause a flat as well.

Put It Back Together
Put just enough air in the tube to make it firm (yes, I said firm) and then slip it back into the tire, which is still off the rim. Next locate the valve hole on the rim and put the valve through it. Then proceed to lace the tire onto the rim one side at a time. It may be necessary to let all the air out of the tube (again) if you're having trouble getting the tire completely on. Whatever you do, don't use a screwdriver or tire lever to get the tire back onto the rim—you'll only puncture the tube and cause yourself another flat. Once the tire is on the rim, pump it up to the pressure recommended by the manufacturer on the side of the tire. Don't go to a gas station to pump up the tire as you'll likely blow it right off the rim.

Reinstall the Wheel
Your wheel is fixed, you're ready to rock. Now, slip it back into the dropouts and hand-tighten the nuts (yes, I said, "hand-tighten the nuts"). If it's the rear wheel make sure you've got the chain on the cog and have the proper chain tension before you give the nuts a few final turns with a wrench. Once the wheel is on, flip your bike back over, make sure that everything is in its place, and you're good to go.

bonus pimply nipple (cap)

Etiquette 101 with Robert Earl

Chopsticks

Don't use your chopsticks to move dishes around on the table.

Don't wave your chopsticks around in the air while you're trying to decide what to eat next, while telling someone a story, or while pointing to the restrooms. Don't use your chopsticks to dig around in the food looking for the best bite—they're not a shovel and you're not on a treasure hunt.

Don't use your chopsticks to scoop earwax or other bodily waste. Do that in the privacy of your own home.

And absolutely no drumming...

Ok, so that covers what NOT to do... as far as figuring out how to use the damn things, you're on your own.

I can't teach you everything.

> Please eat slowly with these, don't run by the pool. And definitely do not point with the choppies.
> Also, don't point your chopsticks at people when you're eating.

Answers for page 45

Pee 1 (water)

Pee 2 (cabbage)

Pee 3 (broccoli)

pee 4 (asparagus)

zenbu
sushi bar & restaurant

(Random trivia only dorks know)

do they know? What are chopsticks made of?

BRADLEY HOLMES

"Chopsticks are lame, except when you want to poke somebody in the eye."

ROOFTOP

"All I gotta say is don't ride your bike or fall off a roof with them in your pocket."

SERGIE VENTURA

"Well, I'd have to say I enjoy a chopstick now and again."

LUKE EGAN

"Chopsticks? Mate, I'm from the land Down Under."

Nicknames: Bad Rad Bumpin' Brad

Home Resort: Squaw Valley, California

Birthplace: Buffalo, New York

Birthdate: Oct. 16, 1969

Brad Holmes:

Resort where you learned to ski: Squaw Valley, California

First time you skied: Four

Where you ski now: Squaw Valley, California

Best results: World Champ

What you like most about skiing: I'm so good at it

Favorite band: Cyndi Lauper

Favorite food: Sushi

Other activities you do besides skiing: Rap and write for *Freeze* magazine

What you wanted to be growing up: A rich skier

In a nutshell, my idol Bradley Holmes brings you some crazy-ass tacos—don't forget the tequila.

flaming baño burritos

Baño Burritos

Brad Holme

Stage #1 — Flaming BAÑO Burritos

* 1 pound chunk Chilean Sea bass
* ½ cup CHILE oil (make sure pan is hotter than a well diggers Ass)
* Cilantro to taste "If you have any"
* 1 shot Taquilla — (gargle shot in mouth and spit in pan ~~and share~~ ~~over left shoulder~~
* ADD Squeeze of Lime and Stir gently, Rapidly and occasionaly

Stage #2

__MAKE Mango Chuntey__

Dice Equal portions of

Mango, Cilantro, Onion, ~~one~~ Jalipaño, Avocodo and add Squeeze of lime. Chill for 30 seconds

Heat CAN Negro frijoles ("Don't beleave the Hype")

Last but Not least — big ASS flour tortillas

Stage #3.

ADD All ingredients Using Common Sence

TAPATÍO

SALSA PICANTE
Hot Sauce
5 FL. OZ. - 148 mL

Frankie "SPF" Barbara:

I tracked down the man the myth the legend "SPF." Otherwise known as Sweet Pussy Frank. You might imagine how a guy can get a name like this—well, yeah, he's sweet and his name is Frank but where does the word "pussy" come from? You might think it has to do with the kittens, but Frank says you are completely wrong. Before we make Frank confess, we just want to let you know you've probably seen Frank at the X Games or the Gravity Games, spiked hair and all, or maybe you've seen the Jones Soda bus cruising across the states. You might have read about some of his adventures in the final pages of Tony Hawk's book *Occupation: Skateboarder*. **Frank, where are we? "Ten more minutes."**

Have you seen his SPF pro model Von Zipper sunglasses? Or maybe heard the tale of when Frank and I dressed up in G-strings and garter belts and surprised Tony and the boys in a restaurant in Richmond, Virginia, during some executive meeting? Well, without further ado, the scoop on the "pussy" in Sweet Pussy Frank. Frank says, "I'll make it short and sweet. I was snowboarding with my friend Lieutenant Mike Gallagher of the Squaw Valley Fire Dept. We were on KT22. After some pretty big storms had passed through, powder abounded and we were feeling courageous. Landings were like pillows so it was time to launch. First Mikey D spins a 360, lands, and waits for me. I get a little cocky, try and launch a twenty-foot backflip, overrotate, and bounce on my neck then somehow to my feet. Mikey D says weak. I say sweet. Then he says I'm a pussy. "Hey yo," he yells, "sweet pussy," whatever—and it stuck ever since. There it is, the myth of Sweet Pussy Frank, and only you know. As for the cooking, this recipe is sweet, and not for pussies.

chicken spedini

ingredients

Chicken breast (skinless and boneless)
3 tablespoons margarine or butter
3 tablespoons olive oil
1 cup Progresso Italian bread crumbs
1/2 cup grated Parmesan cheese
1 lemon (finely chopped, rind only)

what to do

Preheat oven to 375 degrees.
Clean and dry the chicken. Then pound it out until it's just 1/2 inch thick (ok, a hammer ain't
gonna work on this, use a rubber mallet).
Next melt margarine and mix with olive oil in a small, flat bowl. In a separate bowl mix the bread
crumbs, Parmesan cheese, and finely, finely, finely chopped lemon rind.
Dip the pounded-out chicken in the oil/margarine mixture, then in the bread
crumb/cheese/lemon rind mixture. Then place the pounded and coated chicken pieces on a
baking sheet (or a grilling pan if you happen to have one) and bake for 25 to 30 minutes.
A note from Frank: Traditional spedini is rolled after breading, sliced,
and then placed on skewers and grilled.

JONES
SODA CO.

LUKE EGAN: pasta with

Luke has been traveling as a top 20 pro on the world tour for years. He's affectionately known by his peers as Louie. He's come to us with this great recipe all the way from Oz, and claims it was stolen from his X-gal's Italian elders.

cabonasi sausage

ingredients

Cabonasi sausage, thinly sliced
1 whole garlic bulb, chopped
1/2 stick butter
1 pound thick fettuccine noodles, cooked
Tin of peeled tomatoes
Tin of tomato paste
(You can also use Newman's Own tomato sauce. Luke highly recommends it.)

what to do

Pan-fry the cabonasi on low heat with the garlic and butter.
Now put the noodles, the cabonasi, and the red tomato sauce all in one big-ass
   bowl, mix, and serve to the woman or man of your dreams.

LUKE'S BOARD OF CHOICE:

6'4"
X
19 1/8"
X
2 1/2"

SWALLOWTAIL.
SINGLE CONCAVE
TRI-FIN.

how to wax your surfboard

How to Not Get Waxed by a Bad Wax Job...

Ok, you're eyeing your new board and it's looking so perfect you don't even want to lay a finger on it, let alone rub wax all over it. But surfboards aren't pieces of art, and the beauty just gets deeper when you actually put it to use. So, all you need to do is wax it up. Simple, right? Not exactly. A bad wax job will do more than make your board look bad, it will send you into kookdom quicker than putting your leash on the wrong foot. Here's some basic guidelines to keep you from slipping up.

Find a flat, roomy spot to lay your board down, fins on the ground. We recommend your living room in front of your TV. This way you'll be nice and relaxed and less likely to rush through it. But make sure you're not watching E! channel's swimsuit model special or the like—it leads to a tightened grip on the wax and too much pressure applied to the top of the board. Kung fu movies can also cause problems.

Wipe the top of the board free of any foam, dust, or dirt. Don't use the rolled-up sock from under your bed—gooey contents can be disastrous to waxing.

Begin with your base coat wax. Hold one edge of the wax in your hand. (Tip: it's not a beer can, but you can hold it like you would your girlfriend's ATM card when you're sliding it through the little machine at the grocery store check-out stand to buy some beer.)

The Dot Variation, also known as the "Mumps Coat" or "Acne Layer," is a style that has grown more popular lately and involves pressing a corner of the base coat wax against the top of your deck as sort of a guaranteed bump starter. Leave the top eighteen inches or so from the nose of your board down clean—you don't need wax there unless you have the unfortunate problem of being a longboarder. We recommend the DV to the beginner and veteran alike.

Rub the base coat wax in varying circles with light pressure from rail to rail and from your tail to your end point back from the nose (counterclockwise circles in the northern hemisphere, clockwise circles in the southern hemisphere and Santa Cruz).

Now it's on to the second layer. This is where patience pays off. Rub your regular temperature-appropriate wax in circles as you did your base coat. Remember, keep your strokes light, you're not going for release here, just a nice wax job.

You should see nice small bumps all over the deck of your board. Usually half a bar of wax or so should do it. If you've gone through three or four bars, you've put on too much. Scrape it all off and start over.

Now's the good part, sit back and admire your perfect wax job. You'll be the envy of everyone who sees it. The downside: one less excuse next time you take a public tumble at your local beachbreak. And don't commit the cardinal sin of leaving your hard-earned new wax job to bake in the sun in the back of your car because you were too lazy to bring it in. With time and practice, you too can become a Wax Master.

how to fall off a roof

by Mike "Rooftop" Escamilla

Stack cardboard boxes in a pile and be sure to slice the corners out of the boxes so the boxes will fold on impact. When you stack boxes, make sure the area is big enough to hit—I recommend a 20 x 20 area. Feet, that is. Stack boxes on their sides and do not tape them shut. You want the boxes on their sides so they will collapse and the air inside them will break your fall. Use 24-inch cube boxes. You'll need about one row per 10 feet so if you are falling 20 feet you will need two layers. Just to be safe, you must add an additional row. This would put you at three for 20 feet.

Now tape around the whole structure at the bottom row to keep it from splitting down the center. Throw a blanket over the top to soften any sharp corners, and fall away. Try to land on your back or side. Land as flat as possible and this will distribute the weight properly.

If you live, go make my salsa, which you can find on page 46.

If you break your arm, lie and say you saved a dog from getting hit by a car and got hit instead. That will totally get you more points with the ladies. If you tell them you fell off a roof into boxes it may get you deemed the town numnutz. Actually, we do not recommend any of the above, but if you want to be a stuntman, here's a good place to start.

mat HOFFMan:

Where did the idea for this little gem come from?
I was born a choc-o-holic, so my unstoppable sweet tooth (which is about the only tooth Mat has left between the ravages of the Ding Dong Delicious and the world record vert launch) is to blame. Not to mention, before the world got Starbucks and the espresso craze took hold, this breakfast fueled all my good vert sessions.

Who did you first make it for and where?
Me...and me only. If anyone dared to come close or try to take it from me I growled like a nut and scared them away.

What are you eating that keeps you all together?
Ice cream—it's good for the bones, you know.

Countless stitches
Amnesia
Cracked tibia
3 broken toes
6 broken ankles
1 broken fibia
10 screws
1 plate
1 broken rib
1 broken wrist
Reconstructed
  shoulder
3 broken collarbones
25% of collarbone
  removed
16 pinched nerves
  neck and back
Tumor removed
  from leg
2 rotary cuff
  operations

2 broken thumbs
Broken nose
Broken jaw disk
Orthoscopic surgery
  on knee
Bruised knee
Severed leg artery
Very bad concussion
Hit by 4 cars
Severe tendonitis in
  hand, feet & ankles
Chipped teeth
Poor vision
Severe gingivitis
Ingrown toenail
Severe sunburn once

The quicker you stuff it

Ding Dong Delicious

ingredients

Hostess Ding Dongs or King Dons
   (as many as desired)
Godiva Vanilla Caramel Pecan
   ice cream
Chocolate ice cream with swirls
   of golden caramel and
   roasted pecans
Creamy peanut butter
Hershey's Chocolate Milk Mix
1 microwave oven
1 big smile

what to do

Warm the Ding Dongs in the microwave for about 25 seconds. Place the warmed Ding Dongs in the bottom of a bowl, and add the ice cream on top. Microwave the creamy peanut butter to desired consistency (the more time, the more liquid), then add to the dessert. Sprinkle with Hershey's Chocolate Milk Mix and serve!

down your face
the more
you can eat. No etiquette required.

simon tabron:

Straight out of the United Kingdom,

Simon Tabron is known the world over as one of the sweetest, smoothest, and most stylish vert warriors to ever throw a leg over a bike. Known for always going big—like his massive flairs or alley-ooped 900s—and his never-say-die mentality, **the bloke from Liverpool** is always a thrill to watch.

More British than the Queen Mum herself, Simon's latest accomplishments include chugging a steaming cup of Earl Grey tea just before dropping down a vert ramp, landing on the opposite deck, and cracking open a single hardboiled egg with his rear tire. Cheers!

With his insane innovation, dazzling dedication, and supreme support from his loving wife, Simon will most certainly go down as one of the all-time greats in not only the bicycle stunt universe but also the world of **extreme food** preparation. It's a rare occasion to find yourself in the presence of such raw greatness.

Hail, Simon.

ingredients

1 pound minced beef
3 or 4 beef stock cubes
Black pepper
Sugar
Vinegar

Worcestershire sauce
Carrots (as few or as many as you like)
Green beans (same as carrots)
A couple of good-size potatoes
1/4 pound butter
1/4 cup milk
Big handful of grated Cheddar cheese

cottage pie

what to do

First off, brown the minced beef in a large pan and drain off any excess fat. Then add 3 or 4 beef stock cubes, black pepper, a sprinkle of sugar and vinegar to give it bite, and Worcestershire sauce. All of these are added according to taste.

Next you add chopped carrots and chopped green beans. You can precook these or add them raw. It is a matter of taste. I add them raw.

While leaving the beef to simmer, mash the potatoes, mixing them with a little butter, milk, and black pepper.

Take a medium-size oven dish and spread the beef/veg mixture evenly in the dish.

Cover the beef evenly with a thick layer of mashed potatoes.

Before putting the dish into the oven, add a final thin layer of cheese (Cheddar is best).

Put into a preheated oven at 350 degrees for 10 to 15 minutes. Usually, a good way to tell it's ready is when the cheese layer goes crispy.

This is a corn-free recipe

This recipe is a pretty traditional English dish that I have tweaked to my own tastes. It was originally made with lamb and was called Shepherd's Pie, but I'm not a big lamb fan. I have always seen this as comfort food because, when you are super hungry, it only takes about 20 minutes to make and it fills you up like nothing else.

The first time I made it was with my wife, and that is how I make it every time now. You see, I suck at making mashed potatoes so my wife Pippa makes the mash and I make the meat. **When eating Cottage Pie, it is good etiquette to take a little at a time.** If you are still hungry, go back for seconds.

My favorite food is normally Italian like a calzone or a good pizza. Sometimes my favorite food is Tex-Mex chili and sometimes it is Cottage Pie. It all depends where I am and what mood I am in. If I am at a contest I normally gorge myself at Denny's or somewhere like that for breakfast. If I have a long day of riding ahead of me I don't want to have to worry about eating, so I try to eat enough in the morning to last the whole day.

Bucky Lasek:

Maryland Steamed Shrimp

Ingredients
- Shrimp 2.5 pounds
- Old Bay Spice
- fist of Salt (Rock)
- 12oz Vinegar
- 12oz Water
- 12oz Beer
Sauce → Ketchup, Horseradish (away)

BIRDHOUSE SKATEBOARDS · REYNOLDS · MUSKA · SANTOS · SIERRA · LASEK · KLEIN · HAWK

Milkshakes
- Milk
- Ice
- Flavors of your choice (Bananas)
- Chocolate Sauce (syrup)
- Special Chocolate (Coco mix)

ingredients

12 ounces water
12 ounces beer
12 ounces vinegar
Fistful of Old Bay seasoning
Fistful of salt (rock)
2 1/2 pounds shrimp

what to do

Get a big pot for boiling the water, beer, and vinegar all together.

Take the Old Bay seasoning and rock salt and throw them in the pot, and let it all come to a boil.

Get a steamer and place it in the pot; now take your shrimp and place in the steamer, and shut the pot. These babies should chill for about 5 to 8 minutes, soaking up all the spices and the steam.

When this is all done, you are going to take the shrimp out of the steaming situation and peel these bad boys; from here on you're almost ready to eat. Except for one thing—the sauce.

maryland shrimp

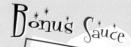
Bucky comes from the East—Maryland, to be specific—and his love of steamed Maryland bay shrimp proves that while you can take the boy out of the East (Bucky and family live in SoCal now), you can't take the East out of the boy.

If you've never had a steaming plate of this East Coast delicacy, I'll tell you there's nothing like 'em. Especially if you have a couple of Bucky's favorite Yuengling lagers on hand. I actually think he stole the recipe from his mom, so if you happen to see Bucky's mom hanging out at the supermarket or wherever, give her a thanks for the finer points of this seafood delicacy.

Is Bucky your real name?
Nah. My first name is Charles, just like my father's. But nobody ever calls me that, everyone calls me Bucky. My mom always called me Bucky because that's what they called my father—wait, did I say that already?

FSHFGT (which means front side heel flip gay twist)

pat parnell: chez le

Patrick Parnell is known as "Chez le Pez" for his exquisite taste and finely tuned nose. After years of traveling to some of the most exotic ports and commentating on the world's best surfers, skaters, and snowboarders, Pat brings a sense of sophistication and grace to X-Cuisine.

From the NBC Gravity Games to the Olympics and the Triple Crown of Surf/Skate/Snow, Pat has been and will be a fixture for years to come. Just make sure to address him as Chez le Pez from now on and be graced with his knowledge of the world from the caves of Singapore to the truffle fields of France.

Chez le Pez is sure to keep you coming back for more.

PEZ BANANA-MAC LOVER

ingredients

1 cup butter
1 cup brown sugar
1 teaspoon cinnamon
1 ounce banana liqueur (if you're a lush, add more if desired)
6 firm (not mushy) bananas cut in half, then lengthwise
    (smaller cuts optional)
1 cup crushed, lightly salted macadamia nuts
6 scoops pure vanilla bean ice cream (don't go cheap here)

what to do

Use large sauté pan (this is very key for slow and even preparation).
Melt butter in pan
Add sugar, cinnamon, and liqueur (stir over low heat).
Stir till mixed.
Heat for a few minutes.
Add bananas.
Sauté lightly till soft.
Scoop ice cream into your best dessert dish.
Gently serve over ice cream.
Sprinkle with macadamia nuts, and voilà!

Bonus Recipe

Morning After Latte
    (aka Russian Cracker)
1 1/2 ounces Grey Goose vodka
    (always use top shelf)
3/4 ounce Kahlua
3/4 ounce whole milk (don't go
    pansy-ass with the nonfat,
    you'll lose flavor)
Nutmeg (if desired)

Mix the vodka and Kahlua
together over crushed ice in
a lo-ball glass, then float the
milk on top. Add sprinkled
nutmeg if desired.

"Chez le Pez"

brian sumner:

B.S., what's the history with this oddball dish?
It was quick and easy and the only thing I knew how to cook! At first me mum thought I was crazy, but soon after people stopped looking at me funny, it began to catch on. Here in the States, all my mates are eating it up. Hell, it's affordable, filling, and it even tastes kind of all right.

Other than Beans on Toast, do you have a favorite food?
Chocolate or pizza, I guess. I'm easy to please.

Do you eat anything special before an event or demo?
Caffeine to get things charged up. I can also highly recommend a chocolate bar.

Why do you always wear black?
I don't know, it's kind of goth. I guess it's the whole miserable English guy syndrome. Even when the temperature hits 107 I still wear black. I just love black.

 70

beans on toast

ingredients
1 can Bush's vegetarian baked beans
3 slices bread (Wonder bread is best)

what to do

Toast the bread in a toaster or oven.
At the same time put the beans in a dish and give 'em 2
minutes in the microwave.
After the bread is nice and crispy, neatly place it in the
middle of the plate, and delicately pour your beans right on the
top. Bingo! You've got beans on toast.
Mmm, mmm, good, mates.

I might even
propose a spot
of tea to go
along with it.

X-iquette

Smashing!
Always speak—or at
least think—with an
English accent while
cooking. Do that and
your food is bound
to turn out perfect.

Heckler: Bavarian Bratwurst with Pasta Marinara

Rock star/brewmaster extraordinaire and all-around extreme athlete, etc., etc.

Bavarian Bratwurst with Pasta Marinara sounds like a mixed bag, I know.

This meal is hearty, low in fat, and quick and easy to make.

Bio tip:

Heckler spends his days of semiretirement snowmobilin', snow skiing, water skiing, surfing, and spending quality time with his bad-ass duck-hunting dog Kreiger.

Gerhard's or O'Dells are preferred but you may have your own favorite. These sausage companies make a fully cooked wurst in a variety of flavors and meats (chicken, turkey, pork, beef). Pick up your flavor off the grocery store's shelf and move on to the pasta.

Italy's most famous, of course! BARILLA! Choose your favorite pasta shape (mostaccioli works killer as does penne rotelli. Now move on to the marinara sauce.

Barilla Marinara sauce. Period. This is shrizen, and key to the whole complexity of flavors.

While you're at the store get yourself a big bag of garden salad with all the shaved carrots and purple cabbage in it. Also get some ranch dressing, and very important, some chile or hot pepper sauce (if you want to call it "pepper sauce" that's yer show). The most crip is good old-fashioned Tabasco brand.

Once in the kitchen just follow the directions on the package and start cooking.

Start the water for the pasta first. When it starts boiling add the pasta and then start the frying pan for the wurst. Cut the wurst down the middle and cook both sides evenly. Here comes the tech part: cook the pasta al dente and drain it in a strainer. Then pour the entire contents of the marinara sauce in the empty but still very hot pot and put the heat on. Stir up the sauce until you see a couple of bubbles and then pour that freshly drained pasta on top and stir it up. This technique has a caramelizing effect on the natural sugars in the sauce and will make yer meal extremely tasty and extra spritzen krippen. Stir and let simmer just a few minutes and then kill the heat.

Meanwhile, you have your salad all mixed up with yer favorite spritzen krippen ranch dressing ready to go. Also meanwhile, yer wurst is ready to be diced up and thrown into the pasta. And also meanwhile, you have a big stein of beer to go along with all of this.

When everything is mixed, cooked, and ready to go, pile it real high on a big plate and let all the foodstuffs just mix together as you go to town.

Don't forget the Tabasco sauce as a condiment for the pasta! A little on the salad won't hurt either.

Save the leftovers in the fridge for quality grinds after a day of blind-side 7's, big mountain descents, or just chillin' on the couch playing Tony Hawk ProSkater 3.

BONUS 32 PAGE SKI HOLIDAY GUIDE

POWDERHOUND

AUSTRALIA AND NEW ZEALAND'S BEST SKI READ

Volume 19 Number 1 $4.95
NZ $8.95 inc. GST

It's Simon Blundell's
FlyingCircus

Zali Steggall's
World Cup Diary
Dan Warbrick
Local Heroes
Inside a Ski Factory
Photo Gallery

Bump**Brothers**
The Amazing Costas

[adrenalin binge]
One week to live [or die] in Queenstown

The **Best Ski Buys** of '95

ISSN 1321-7003

9 771321 700009   01

73

Kevin Staab: spicy

Staab-o-licious

If you've ever had a midlife crisis, had a pair of Half Cabs when they first came out, or were a reader of *Thrasher* magazine in the mid-80's, the mere mention of Kevin Staab brings back the long, scraggly hair, the big ramps, fast plants, and post-punk Glam Wave rock. Staab's been on the skate scene for twenty-five years, kickin' it with Tony Hawk and watching as skateboarding evolved from the sport of Dogtown delinquents to a made-for-TV extreme sport. All the while, Staab's been there keeping it oh-so-real.

Things are still rockin' for Kevin, so much so that pro skating is just a small part of the picture. He flipped the switch on his own clothing company last year, A42, he manages the Hawk shoes team, and he definitely spends his share of time around the BBQ perfecting his own special, Staab-o-licous turkey burgers.

Where did it come from?
Many, many summer nights at the BBQ experimenting with everything and anything in the house. I made it for my girlfriend Vanessa (it musta been good because she's now my beautiful wife) and any friends that happened to be hanging out on special summer nights. Here's the deal: you can't be scared or afraid to experiment with food. You've got to go big—even if you think it could be a bomb. Regardless of how the food turns out, it's tons of fun to cook with friends and loved ones. Do I sound like someone's mother on the cooking channel or what?

Got a favorite food?
I love making chicken tacos, chocolate chip and golden graham pancakes, and orange peanut butter bow tie pasta.

Do you eat anything special before an event or demo?
Big cup of coffee and some cereal. Or Dr Pepper and a peanut butter and jelly sandwich. Whatever happens to be on hand, but I gotta say that I love a nice plate of eggs Benedict and a foamy mocha.

I'd love to go on all day, but I got to go skate now. So enjoy. I would like to say hi to my wife, Vanessa, and to Ethan John Sebastian Staab. When you're old enough to read this, you better be ready to cook me dinner.

74

sweet turkey burgers

ingredients

Garlic
Green pepper
Red pepper
Mushrooms
Ground turkey
Pepper jack cheese
Hawaiian sweet bread
Cooking spray or vegetable oil
Don't forget the A-1
Lettuce
Tomato
Onion
Avocado (if desired)

what to do

Dice up your veggies into little pieces because you're going to mix them with the ground turkey.

Combine ground turkey with your veggies and mix well.

Get that barbecue rocking.

Slice up your favorite cheese into about 2-inch squares about 1/4 inch thick. (Pepper Jack is good because spicy goes nice with sweet bread.)

Roll up mixture into small patties and smash them down about 1/2 inches to fit the Hawaiian bread. (A little Pam or oil on your hands will keep the mixture from sticking as you roll these little gems.)

Put the patties on a plate and get them to the 'cue.

Cook about 3 to 5 minutes per side depending on how hot the 'cue is. Lay on the cheese, and heat until cheese is melted. Toast your buns on the 'cue, add a little dab of A-1 and your choice of lettuce, tomato, onion, and garlic and you're ready to feast!

＊ extra
Staab-a-mole
(Make a lot of this stuff and you can have a snack with some chips while you're cooking.)

Cut avocado in half and squeeze out the good stuff.
Add a little lemon pepper.
Add a little ranch dressing, or sour cream.
Add a little squirt of fresh lime, and some hot salsa.
Mash it up with a fork.

now go hang out with your friends and eat.

how to kevin staab hair info

How to keep your hair lookin' good
by Resident Fashion Expert Kevin Staab

SOAP

Soap works well for short hair as it keeps a nice messy look. Get hands wet, lather up your favorite soap, slop it in, give a little run through with a dry towel and presto! (I think I started experimenting with this in the early '80s.)

GELATIN

Ok, don't use Jell-O, this is different.

Mix this stuff up with warm water like it says on the package, mix a handful evenly through your hair, lean over, and crank a blow dryer on full speed.

Move the blow dryer back and forth until you feel the hair gelatin goop start to dry and get a little stiff. Then, depending on the look you want, lean from side-to-side as you're blow drying and create a nice style. After it's completely dry it feels like a bunch of little rubber snakes. Kind of a mini-dread look.

TOOTHPASTE

Yes, friends, it's good for the teeth and it's good for styling short hair. Four out of five punks recommend it!

Put a little of your favorite toothpaste in your hands, rub 'em together a bit, and apply it to your head. Add more as needed. As a bonus, this washes out easily.

OLD LADY HAIRSPRAY TIP

For hair that's not going to move until a monsoon drops on your head, use Aqua Net, the stuff in the pink can. This stuff has never let me down.

POMADE

Sweet Georgia Brown: soft easy-to-manage pomade, good for a messy look. Black & White: a nice medium for a firmer spike look. Dax: the stiffest of the pomade, great for spikes of up to 2 inches.

HAIR GEL

Old reliable. I've long been a fan of LA Style gel. Always works for a good spike look. Apply it generously, lean to one side, blow dry. Check it out periodically to make sure it's standing as you like it. The great thing about this stuff is as it's drying it's still easy to sculpt with your fingers or a hair pick.

Bonus Color Dying Tip:

Use Punky Color for the best, brightest color possible. Bleach your own hair before using Punky Color to get the brightest, most vibrant colors.

76

In the Kitchen with *Robert Earl*

kitchen tools

not too sweet....
use caution blending...

Six You Cannot Live Without

Aluminum foil

Can opener

Cheese grater

Colander (for draining pasta)

Wooden spoons

The Barebones Basics

Cutting board (wood sounds great, but plastic will do just fine)

Ice cream scooper

Measuring cups (set of four)

Measuring spoons

Mixing bowls (set of three)

Plastic wrap

Rubber spatula

Tongs

Vegetable peeler

Whisk

Wine opener

Highly Optional

Citrus juicer

Cooling rack

Food processor

Plastic storage containers with tight-fitting lids

Rolling pin

Salad spinner

Toaster oven

Toothpicks

Waxed paper

Tom Burt: Bear-Poo

Tahoe native Tom Burt—he's the big mountain guy riding the big lines, where there's no one likely to see him, like the time he rode off the 20,000-foot top of Mt. McKinley. Not one to spend a Saturday night in a high-end sushi bar, Tommy has collected some serious culinary tricks all the way from the Alaskan outback to the far Far East.

Once in a while even a free-ride pioneer and absolute big mountain hell-man like Burt needs to take a break. So we caught up with him relaxing Baja-style at his summer hideaway just off the Pacific coast. By the time we found him, he'd had enough of the local tuna tacos and mangoes, so he pulled a page from his Russian family album for **an internationally** *orgasmic* **treat: Shashlik!**

Where did it come from?
An old family recipe from Russia.

Did you learn it while in a faraway land or are you taking credit for your grandma's favorite cookies?
It came from the homeland of my mom's side of the family.

Who did you first make it for and where?
A barbecue birthday party for my twenty-fifth at my house in Kings Beach, California. I made it for all my friends who showed up.

Is it the only thing you know how to make?
It is a good way to make your friends' stomachs happy.

What's your favorite food?
Whatever is on the plate in front of me. I am not a picky eater. I like food. Ma Burt's cheesecake rules, though. Maybe I will have to follow up with that recipe.

Do you eat anything special before an event or demo?
Anything. I just shove it down my throat.

X-iquette

Know how to set a table and what fork or spoon to use and know its purpose.

It's ok to eat things like chicken with your fingers.

stew (shashlik)

PIG FEST

BURT

ingredients

1 leg of lamb
3 to 4 bunches of
    green onions
Salt
Pepper
6 to 8 lemons

what to do

Cut leg of lamb into kabob-size chunks of meat.
    Put it in a bowl. Chop onions in half and add to
    lamb. Add a little salt and pepper. Cut lemons in
    half and squeeze juice onto meat. Mix together
    and then place the wrung-out lemon halves on top of the meat. Then cover and let marinate for 4
    hours minimum. The longer it marinates the better. You can even leave it overnight.

About an hour before you're ready to serve the Shashlik, fire up the BBQ. Once you've got the charcoal
    good and warm, make sure the coals are in a nice pile in the center of the grill.

A few minutes before you're ready to grill your Shashlik, pull the lamb mixture from the refrigerator
    and slide chunks of lamb onto wooden skewers and cook over the hot coals. Leave the meat on the
    grill between 10 and 20 minutes, turning a few times to ensure that the lamb cooks evenly.

While the Shashlik is grilling, drain and place the green onions that were marinating with the lamb on
    the grill too, then arrange them on a platter. Once the skewers of lamb are grilled to your liking,
    stack 'em on the platter and go to town.

how to fold napkins

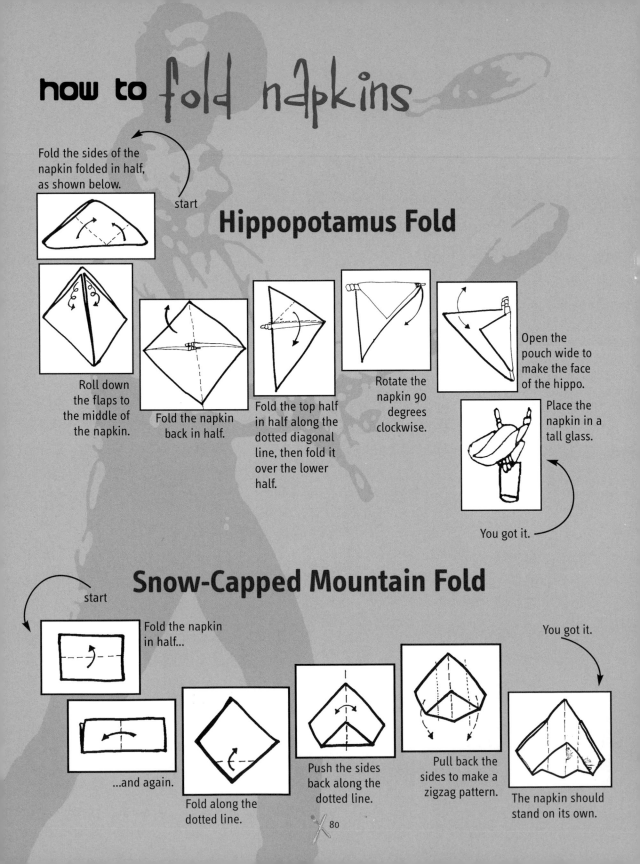

Fold the sides of the napkin folded in half, as shown below.

start

Hippopotamus Fold

Roll down the flaps to the middle of the napkin.

Fold the napkin back in half.

Fold the top half in half along the dotted diagonal line, then fold it over the lower half.

Rotate the napkin 90 degrees clockwise.

Open the pouch wide to make the face of the hippo.

Place the napkin in a tall glass.

You got it.

Snow-Capped Mountain Fold

start

Fold the napkin in half...

...and again.

Fold along the dotted line.

Push the sides back along the dotted line.

Pull back the sides to make a zigzag pattern.

You got it.

The napkin should stand on its own.

80

Etiquette 101 with Robert Earl

Your New Best Friend: The Napkin

Ah yes, the napkin has saved many a sloppy eater and there's no doubt it'll save your bacon some day, so treat it with all the care and respect you show to your X-Box.

When you sit down at the table, your napkin will either be set in a goofy little tent on your plate or off to the side of the plate. But which one is yours? It should be the one on the left. The first thing you do when you've sat down at the table is to take the napkin from your place setting and to put it on your lap. Even if you're in a rib joint on the south side of town, don't tuck the napkin into your shirt—leave it on your lap (except if you're flying in an airplane, then the shirt tuck is fine).

It shouldn't be used to blow your nose in or to clean your fingernails with, wipe behind your ears, or soak the blood off your elbow. A napkin is a napkin is a napkin and it's always for wiping food from around your mouth.

So you're doing pretty well with your meal, but nature calls or maybe there's a girl at table ten who you'd like to get a closer look at. What do you do with your napkin when you jump up from the table? Stuff it in your buddy's soup? No. When you get up, pull the napkin from your lap, put it on the seat of your chair, and push your chair into the table so that it's not sticking out in everyone's way.

When everyone has finished with the meal and you're ready to move on to bigger and better things, get up from the table, drop your napkin back on the seat of the chair, push the chair back into the table, and say goodbye to your new best friend.

Napkins, napkins, napkins... read the detailed information closely, but here's what I think...this is absolutely the easiest way to look like you know what you're doing. Sit down IMMEDiately and put the darn thing in your lap. The worst is to sit down and see a poor lad sit there with his napkin on the table for the whole meal. So remember to read closely for all the insight to your new best friend the napkin. Good luck with the folding lesson. Linen, not paper... ok?

(Random trivia only dorks know)

do they know? Can you fold a napkin into a hat?

TOM BURT

"I really enjoy folding these in the shape of Mt. McKinley."

BIG B

"Did you know that hole in the airplane napkin is for the button on your shirt?"

ANDREW CRAWFORD

"Napkins bore me. I'd much rather burn out on one."

MIKE PARSONS

"I love making the standing wave with mine. Then I like to kiss Nicole, after wiping my mouth, of course."

taj Burrow: Weetabix

His mom and dad are both incredible surfers from the States, so he's got the California style wired (including his love of Mexican food).

But have a beer with him and you'll see that Sabo-Taj learned a lot about Aussie pride growing up in Western Australia. His big air and rough cut style have made Burrow one of the great new surfers firing up the scene.

T.B., looks like you're packin' some serious Aussie heat today.
Yep. My recipe is the very simple but very special breakfast of banana and honey on Weetabix, and of course a few slices of Vegemite toast. The classic Australian breakfast.

Where did it come from?
Come on, I think every Aussie kid was raised on this breakfast! I don't even have Australian parents and I was brought up like this so you know it's the standard! My parents are from California, and I guess serving this to your kid is a prerequisite for immigrating to Oz!

Who did you first make this for?
I only make this meal for myself, you wouldn't make this for anyone until you had a kid of your own, I guess. I have been known to eat this meal for lunch or even dinner because it's so quick and healthy and tastes so good, but it's really best when eaten for breakfast.

Where do the hottest girls live?
Argentina from what I've heard, but from my experience France has really beautiful women, so I'll go with France.

Favorite surf trip ever?
Mentawai Islands, Indonesia—I was lucky to go to a cool place with a kick-ass crew!

with banana and honey
& vegemite toast

ingredients

5 or 6 Weetabix
1 ripe banana
1 jar honey
1 carton milk

what to do

Pretty basic here. You start by putting roughly five Weetabix in a cereal bowl. Next, select a ripe banana from a bunch, peel it, and slice it into small pieces.
   I like to peel one side of the banana off and cut it with my spoon while it's still in the other half of its peel. Using the spoon amounts to limiting this whole recipe to one utensil, which obviously saves time when it comes to washing up!
Put the sliced banana on top of the Weetabix and smother it with as much honey as you can stand. Then add milk. I usually like about a half-filled cereal bowl in order to avoid what is commonly called soggy Weetabix! Our motto around here is Never Eat Soggy Weetabix (NESW), also known as North East South West! Haaaaa.

Vegemite Toast

2 pieces of bread (or as much as you can eat)
1 stick butter
1 jar of Vegemite

Start with a few slices of your favorite bread (mine is a soy/linseed special). Next, toast the toast for as long as you like. Then, smother as much butter on it as you can possibly feel comfortable with.
Ok, here's the key to top-shelf Vegemite Toast: just thinly spread your Vegemite around your butter-soaked toast. In a lifetime of experimentation, I've found that a small amount of Vegemite spread very thinly works the best.

What the hell is Vegemite anyway?

All you non-Australian kids are wondering what in the hell Taj puts on his toast. Well, depending on where you're from, Vegemite is either mother's milk or a foul-smelling black paste.

Like Australia itself, Vegemite is a fairly recent concoction. It was created in the early 1920's when an Australian cheesemaker started buying up spent brewers' yeast with the idea of making an Aussie version of Marmite (a yeast extract paste popular in England). A chemist at the cheese company, Dr. Cyril P. Callister, is the one who has gone down in the history books for actually turning the yeast waste into what an entire continent now knows and loves as Vegemite.

Being an Australian chemist and not an American marketing guy, Callister didn't have a name for his new spread, so he and the company turned it over to the Australian public, who came up with the name Vegemite.

The rest, as they say, is history. Ever since Vegemite gained popularity in the first half of the century, Australia's Happy Little Vegemites have been saying "Pass the Vegemite please, Mum."

Although the stuff has never caught on in this country (I guess peanut butter and jelly is pretty damn hard to beat), the name and trademark for Vegemite was eventually purchased by the American company Kraft Foods. True to form, we Americans simply bought what we couldn't understand.

83

...it's a good idea to make something

Jamie mosberg:

with a French name if you're looking to get the ball rolling with that special lady.

First of all, for the record, Jamie Mosberg is the man behind the lens and has written and produced stuff you've been watching for years. He shot *Pickled* and numerous other action-sport epics, and if you'll notice his spread, he's been known to go way above vert. Mosberg is otherwise know as Mouse or, to his close friends, the Moose, and has stepped it up with this magical treat.

Jamie, what's the story with the French twist on ceviche?
It came from Tahiti, so it's at least partially French. Tanya says it means raw fish, but I thought it meant coconut fish. Whatever. Every restaurant in Tahiti serves it cold like salad. While it's really cheap here—as cheap as French fries are in the States—it can be pretty spendy in America.

Who did you first make it for?
I made it for a date, she loved the name and kept saying it with a French accent—it was real sexy. So, it's a good idea to make something with a French name if you're looking to get the ball rolling with that special lady.

What do you eat to power you through a super long edit?
Cookies, cookies, and more cookies.

Mouse's painted living room wall.

POISSON CRU CRAWFISH

ingredients

2 pounds extra fresh ahi tuna
15 to 20 fresh limes,
    depending on size
5 to 7 thin slices ginger
2 to 4 cloves garlic
1 or 2 cans coconut milk
1 onion

8 cucumbers
Few pinches salt
Dash pepper
1/4 cup loosely packed
    FRESH basil
4 to 5 tomatoes (optional)
1 to 2 carrots (optional)

what to do

First, slice up the ahi into small cubes—probably about 1/4 inch square.
Drop 'em into a big bowl.
Cut the limes into halves and squeeze all the juice you can onto the fish.
When the juice and the fish get together, the fish will start to change color, this means the acid is actually cooking it—a good thing!
Mix the fish and juice up really, really well, but be gentle with the fish to preserve the taste.
Slice the ginger and crush the garlic and throw it into the mix.
Stir one more time.
Crack open the coconut milk and add it to the fish/lime/ginger/garlic mix.

Stir again, mixing everything really well.
Dice up one onion, add it, and stir again.
Peel the eight cucumbers, cut into quarter-sized pieces, and add to the mix.
Stir again.
Add the salt, pepper, and basil and stir until you're blue in the face.
Let sit for about an hour and then bon appétit!
The Poisson Cru is better the second day than right when you make it because it's had a chance to soak up all the flavors.
Make this for a lovely lady, give her some rap with a French accent, and you're in.

85

Movies that Mouse has produced and directed.

Born and bred in San Clemente, California, Mike "Snips" Parsons has surfed some of the biggest waves ever ridden. Tired of surfing waves that people already knew about, Snips ventured a hundred miles off the California coast and discovered his own private big wave spot—Cortes Bank. And boy, has it paid off. After pulling down $60,000 for winning the Nissan XXL contest, Snips sold the rights to his life story for a cool six figures.

How in the hell do Todos Tacos fit into the picture? Todos Santos Island just off the northern coast of Baja is for sure one of the most infamous big wave breaks in the world; a spot about an hour off the mainland where waves break over 20 feet on a small day. Having surfed the biggest days anyone has seen there, Parsons owns the Todos break, but it was one unlucky day that led to the fascinating discovery of this long-lost secret recipe.

"I was with a bunch of the guys. It was only about a 15-foot wave kind of day, but all of a sudden this monster set comes rolling through. I absolutely couldn't believe my eyes. I turned to get out of there because I had crappy positioning and didn't want to get pounded by the other guys, but I couldn't make it away. It was one of the longest drops of my life—and then it was lights out! I didn't make the drop, was held under, broke my board and got washed in all the way to the island. After crawling up on shore I lay down and tried to pull myself together. A cactus was right next to me and underneath it was a small piece of yellowed paper with some Spanish scribbling on it. I stuffed it in my sleeve and caught a ride back out to the channel on the Jet Ski. Done for the day, I stripped down on the boat and out popped the paper. The driver snatched it up and asked me if I knew what I had found. Hell, I barely knew what planet I was on, let alone what was written on that paper. He laughed and said, 'Miguel, do you know that this is the long-lost recipe for Todos Tacos and the island's special sauce! I will translate it and we will all eat like kings tonight thanks to your bad luck today.' And the rest is history."

mike parsons: todos

tacos

ingredients

5 pieces of fresh snapper
3 eggs, beaten
2-ounce special mexi seasoning mix
   package (spices, pepper, salt)
1 cup flour
Olive oil
2 limes
3 fresh tomatoes
1 fresh mango
Fresh clump of cilantro
12 flour or corn tortillas

what to do

Cut fish into nice strips, dip in the egg,
   then proceed to dunk into your mexi
   flour seasoning sauce. Once all pieces
   have been breaded let them rest for 2
   minutes while your frying pan heats
   up and the 1/8 to 1/4 inch of oil
   begins to crackle.
Simultaneously you'll be slicing your
   limes, dicing your tomatoes and
   mango, and mincing your cilantro.
   Get that prepared and place it on the
   counter next to you, squeeze in lime
   juice. Go ahead and toss in the fish.
   Make it golden brown, no longer than
   4 minutes each side. Slightly heat and
   brown your tortillas, and you are
   ready to roll.

Food for two

Bonus Recipe

Guacamole. This is the recipe that
Snips dug up on Todos Island
while waiting to be rescued. It is
believed to originate from the
first-ever taco stand in Baja.

2 avocados
Tons of garlic
Cilantro
Fresh salsa
Salt and pepper
Lime juice

Put in bowl.
Smash the shit out of it.
Go splurge for some fresh flour chips
   from your favorite Mexi restaurant.
   Give the busboy a few bucks.
No Doritos.

grease fire

"BIG B"

chris burke: rice

A professional surfer from back in the day, the always super sweet Big B made the cover of *Surfing* magazine back in '86. Kids, this dude is beyond legendary and he is none other than the man behind the phrase "How ya livin'?" Big B, named by his parents as Chris Burke, is also the founder of the Endangered Concepts Society, a renegade artists group.

His move out of the water and into the boardroom was flawless as he retired from the life of a pro surfer and jumped in as one of the founding members of the Arnette sunglasses startup crew. Using his marketing skills and worldwide connections, he blew the thing up in a mere two-year period. His latest creation, Von Zipper eyewear, has gained momentum as a global brand after barely a year in existence!

His photography and ads are taking the country by storm, and yet this creative guru has blessed us with a little morsel, from the archives of the Endangered Concepts Society, so keep this one in reserve for very special occasions.

And when you see "Biggs-Z." as his friends call him, make sure to ask him, "How ya livin'?"

"How ya livin'?"

ingredients

- 2 fresh sweet corn stalks (cut kernels off)
- 4 carrots, sliced
- 2 red bell peppers, diced
- 2 scrambled eggs
- 2 cups long grain rice
- 2 cups water
- 2 teaspoons balsamic vinaigrette
- 4 tablespoons soy sauce

what to do

Mix all ingredients in rice cooker.
Set time for 55 minutes.
Go surfing.
Open a cold Steinlager.

Life Is Good.

Life Is Good.

smoothies

super rainbrah smoothie

2 to 3 cups ice
2 bananas
2 to 3 mint leaves
1 tablespoon raw sesame tahini
1 organic kale leaf (cut stem out)
1 tablespoon spirulina powder

what to do

Get ready to rock Rainbrahs. Dump it all in a blender, blend it on high until the whole mix is smooth and creamy. Pour into a glass, garnish the green goo with a mint leaf, and power up.

bunny hop smoothie

1 or 2 cups ice
1/2 cup carrot juice
1/2 cup apple juice
Half a fresh lemon
Healthy pinch of shaved fresh ginger

what to do

This is a good healthy one that I found at a super crusty health food store in northern California. Drop it all in a blender (squeeze the lemon juice into the blender, don't blend the whole thing), blend it on high until everything is well blended, and enjoy.

creamsicle smoothie

1 1/2 cups cantaloupe chunks
1 cup orange juice
1/2 cup vanilla yogurt
1 tablespoon honey
1 teaspoon vanilla

what to do

This is a sweet, but healthy one good for the summertime. Blend it all in a blender until smooth and orange-a-licious. Keep in mind that if you don't drink this one quickly you might have to stir it since it can separate and look kinda gross.

Bonus Recipe

Tony Montana's Say Goodnight Smoothie

2 to 3 cups ice
1 8-ounce can WhoopAss
2 shots Grey Goose vodka (for the kids over 21)
1/2 fresh lemon
2 to 3 fresh mint leaves

You'll want to have a professional mixologist do this one up for you. Sip from a gold-rimmed rocks glass, then say "Goodnight to the bad guy."

FOOD for thought

with *Robert Earl* ooo

oops! i coulda had a veggiesmoothie' veggie smoothie

1 1/2 cups V8 juice
1 cup ice
1/2 cup fresh carrot juice
1 teaspoon fresh lemon juice
1 teaspoon Tabasco (or to taste)
5 to 10 spinach leaves
1 sprig parsley

what to do

This is a good one for just about anybody, as you can find these ingredients in any good grocery store any time of the year. Dump everything in a blender except the parsley and blend the heck out of it. Use as much Tabasco or other hot sauce as you like/can stand. Garnish with a nice sprig of parsley and have your way with it.

uncle jed's kentucky fried smoothie

2 cups ice
1 12-ounce can RC Cola
1 king-size Snickers bar (go for the regular size if you're watching your weight)
1 tablespoon Hershey's syrup (or to taste)

what to do

You've got two options here. You can dump it all in a blender, blend until smooth, and drink it down while watchin' the Springer show or you can chug the RC, eat the Snickers, suck the syrup out of the bottle, and stick the ice down your sister's friend's top. Either way, Uncle Jed's Kentucky Fried Smoothie is sure to please.

anthony frank hawk:

the bird bagel

Tony Hawk. The man owns skating like Jordan owns hoops. All of you know the skinny kid on the ramp pullin' 900's like a drunk monkey, but what you don't know is T. Hawk the family man. That's right, between creating new tricks, running the Hawk empire, and playing video games for hours on end, this southern California skater makes a whole lot of time for his three boys.

Just like you'd expect from the sport's biggest innovator, Hawk even pushes the limits in the kitchen. Sure, it doesn't always work out, but Tony claims that no one has ever died from his cooking. Well, at least not yet.

While holding Keagan and watchng Spencer in a nearby rocker, Tony explains that the Bird Bagel is his oldest son Riley's favorite family treat. Since his wife, Erin, needs a little extra sleep in the mornings after chasing the kids all day (including Tony), they both agree that the Bird Bagel is a lifesaver. "The first time he made it," Erin said, "I had no idea what he was doing in the kitchen. Now Riley won't eat anything else in the morning." But she was quick to add that "Make no mistake. Tony didn't win me over with his cooking or his skating. It was his sweetness and dedication to me and the family. But 900's and those Bird Bagels are certainly a plus..."

We caught up with the world's greatest skater in his So-Cal castle kitchen.

Where's the Bird Bagel from?
It was inspired by my numerous visits to bagel shops and a quest for the ultimate breakfast sandwich. It is also my son's favorite no matter what time of day, so I've perfected the technique.

I guess that tells us who you first made it for?
Yep, I made it for my son, per his request when we didn't have time to go out for breakfast one day. It was a gamble as to whether he would like it or not—first because he's a kid, and more importantly because I DON'T COOK. It turned out to be a success, and he now prefers mine over all the big guys—Bonjour, Bruegger's, and Einstein Bros.

You've traveled the world and eaten every kind of food imaginable, what's your favorite?
Japanese food. Namely, Zaru soba (cold buckwheat noodles with dipping sauce). I'm also big on sushi, stuff like California handrolls, Unagi (BBQ'd eel), shrimp tempura, and tuna sashimi, all with obscene amounts of wasabi.

Do you eat anything special before an event or demo?
A #1 combo at In-N-Out.

How many times a week do you cook vs. eating out?
I eat out at least once a day. Breakfast is usually at home, lunch is always out and dinner varies (depending on whether my wife, Erin, feels like cooking).

95

tony Hawk's bird bagel

ingredients

1 egg
1 shredded Jack & Cheddar cheese mix
1 bagel (preferably plain)

what to do

Find a microwave-safe bowl approximately the same diameter as a bagel. "We have perfect-size Tupperware bowls in our house, but I have no idea where they came from."

Crack the egg over the bowl and pour it in. If you manage to not spill any egg outside the bowl or get any bits of shell in it, then you are a Bird Bagel Prodigy. Scramble it.

Sprinkle cheese over the egg, covering the top completely with a thin layer.

Split the bagel and stick it in the toaster.

Heat the egg in the microwave on high for a minute and a half.

Wait patiently—have some coffee or juice. Now is a good time to throw the egg shell away, put the cheese back, and clean the fork you used to scramble the raw egg. Never risk salmonella for haste.

Use the freshly cleaned fork to remove the egg and cheese creation from the bowl and place it on the bagel. Work on the timing of toasting versus egg cooking so that both come out hot (cold eggs are nasty).

Cut the Bird Bagel in half and consume. Eat it in your car if you are in a hurry. Don't forget to pick up a vanilla café au lait or vanilla iced blended if there is a Coffee Bean and Tea Leaf on your way.

X-iquette

Never eat at a Chinese place with the word "Golden," "Panda," "Palace," "Gate," "Dragon," or "Express" in the name.

Etiquette 101 with *Robert Earl*

The Dinner Table and How to Set It

Sounds like bunk and trivial info. However, this will come in handy, and may even score you some points (or get you laid), when:

You are having a dinner party and want to look sweet (James Bond style).

You are helping your girlfriend's parents set up their dinner party (your gal's mum will be thoroughly impressed).

You bail on school to become a busboy— now you're qualified.

See diagram.

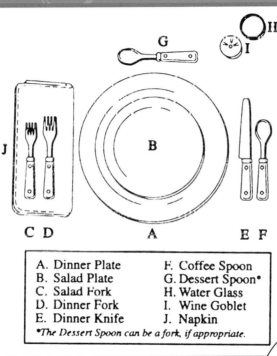

A. Dinner Plate
B. Salad Plate
C. Salad Fork
D. Dinner Fork
E. Dinner Knife
F. Coffee Spoon
G. Dessert Spoon*
H. Water Glass
I. Wine Goblet
J. Napkin

The Dessert Spoon can be a fork, if appropriate.

Did you know that animals on the outside of a herd always get eaten first? If not, now you know, and the same goes for eating utensils. Always start with the outside fork/spoon and work your way in. So if you get some kind of weird roughage that looks like a salad, take the outside fork and dig in. If you get to dessert and have only a knife left, you're screwed, although this rarely happens.

Word to the wise: Never let your knife hit the table once it's touched your food. And never, NEVER use your hands UNLESS you're eating Mike Parsons' Todos Tacos (more on these delectable treats on page 86).

do they know?

(Random trivia only dorks know)

Why is one fork bigger than the other?

SHANE DORIAN

"Well, I think one fork is bigger than the other because doing dishes is fun and when it is really formal it lends you more options."

WILLY SANTOS

"Because you should have two forks in case one doesn't work, or you drop one on the ground."

BENJI WEATHERLY

"Duh, one is for your vegetables and one is for your meat. What? Wait, I think I'm correct, psyche..."

BUCKY LASEK

"I really don't know. I usually use a spork, which is a spoon and a fork and for Maryland crabs I use a hammer and my fingers."

97

ANDY HETZEL: SPICY

shrimp barbecue

Where did the recipe come from ?
I'm a barby master, and the 'cue is my canvas.
I taught myself from years of practice and
drinking cold malt beverages alongside my
friend the gas grill.

Who did you first make it for and where?
Just cooking for my girls, or my roommates who
are usually borderline useless.

Barbecue tips with Hetzel:

- Gas grills all the way. Gas provides a steady flame and is very dependable. Coals can be finicky and tough. Never overcook your meat; take it off and check it to be sure. Tinfoil can be a great help in cooking anything from garlic to veggies and everything in between.
- Always heat the grill and scrape before use; it's always good to have a hot grill to throw meat on.
- Sear both sides of beef for a minute or two and then turn grill down for the rest of your cooking experience.
- Have the remainder of your meal ready at the same time your barbecue is. Timing is the key.
- I highly recommend Schillings Montreal steak seasoning.
- Never cross-contaminate your meats—no mix of chicken and beef. This could lead to death or bad gas. Beware.

andy Ketzel: spicy shrimp barbecue

ingredients

12 medium or large shrimp, peeled and
cleaned
1 can of pineapple slices
Teriyaki sauce
Olive oil
Salt
Pepper
Schillings Montreal steak
seasoning

what to do

Marinate in the morning
for afternoon 'cue or the
night before.
Put the shrimp in a bowl.
Add pineapple juice from the can.
Add teriyaki sauce.

You can cook this either in tinfoil or on skewers. I prefer the tinfoil for a juicier shrimp, and it's easier to cook with in general. Add a good amount of olive oil, salt, pepper, and the key ingredient, Schillings Montreal steak seasoning. Place the shrimp in tinfoil and cook over a low to medium heat for roughly 8 to 10 minutes, flipping twice. Check shrimp after 8 minutes. If they're pink, they're done.

Anaheim Chiles with Feta
Cut chiles lengthwise and empty out the seeds. Rub in olive oil to prevent sticking and burning. Stuff feta in chiles, packing fully. Close the chiles by hand and keep them closed. The key here is not to burn the chiles too bad. Cook on low to medium heat, the same as the shrimp. You just want to melt the cheese. Cook for 5 to 9 minutes, moving around a few times to cook the chiles completely.

Filets
Get a couple nice filets and season with salt, pepper, and garlic. The steaks should be put on a hot grill and seared on each side briefly; then turn the heat down—cook roughly 5 to 10 minutes, flipping once if you're good. I recommend rare—to medium rare, don't overcook your steak. It's a sin. Potatoes, just bake 'em. It's easy. Beans, I just can't say enough about beans. I love them. Baked are my favorite (Bush's original). You can't go wrong. You can overcook beans, though, so start them late in your prep process. Cook them on the stove.

Etiquette 101 with Robert Earl

Soup du Jour

Soup, soup, soup. It comes in all different shapes and sizes—hot, cold, meat, no meat, vegetables, or broth. Usually a soup spoon is rounder and wider than a teaspoon so as to fit more on, and even bigger if you're drinking down some broth-based soup.

Soups are all eaten the same way. Hold your spoon in your right or left hand. Then, moving the spoon away from you, go in for a spoonful. Remember to keep your momentum moving forward toward the front or top of the bowl. Now tip the spoon back into your mouth from the side. Don't go for it head-on. No slurping.

Okay, if you need to take a break, rest the spoon in the bowl, not outside of it, and don't ever let the spoon touch the table once it's been in the bowl.

When you are all done, put the spoon on the plate or saucer and you are good to go.

Soup. Oh, how a bowl of soup can make a rainy day sunny and a cold day go away. I never really knew what to do with the spoon, though. But now you know. Try not to slurp and make sure to really stock up on soup in the pantry. You can live on it for weeks. So practice the soup technique while you're enjoying your favorite bowl of split pea or chicken noodle.

do they know?
(Random trivia only dorks know)

Wait, what? A spoon?

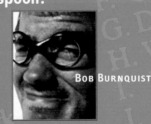

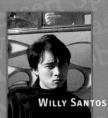

SAL
"Are you kidding? Of course the soup spoon stays in the bowl when you are eating..."

BAM
"I drink right out of the bowl."

BOB BURNQUIST
"It's all about organic tomato soup and eating with a bamboo spoon. Yes, organic."

WILLY SANTOS
"I am really backing the spoons they use in Japanese and Chinese restaurants. Those are sweet. And I own a sushi place, so I love miso."

Etiquette 101 with Robert Earl

Sticky Situations

What to do.

Every once in a while you'll need to be prepared to get out of a sticky situation with the elegance, grace, and charm of an *X-treme Cuisine* eater.

You ate something that could be making you feel gassy. Squeeze your buns as tight as you can, don't call attention to yourself. If you choose this option, keep it up for as long as possible till the gas passes. Another option is to excuse yourself from the table and head for the nearest bathroom. Make sure to stay away long enough so nothing trails you back to the table.

You get a piece of bone or a bite of something really nasty that makes you want to barf. Well don't just spit it back up into your napkin; remember, your napkin is your new best friend. Slowly and calmly bring your fork up to your mouth and do a reverse bite. Place the item on the tip of your fork, then back on your plate. Hide with garnish, and no one will ever know a thing.

What if you can't stand the food being served to you? It brings back visions of *The Exorcist,* or your grandma used to make you eat it when you were young. Now you are old enough to realize you do not like fruitcake. Well, now is the time to suddenly become allergic to certain food items. Just say, "No thank you," and let it pass on by.

> Sticky situations. We've all been there—bad gas, burping, bad food. All I gotta say is divert all attention to the passing blimp. Divert, divert divert, and remember everyone's been embarrassed before; don't let it get you down. Just keep rockin', and be all sweet.

do they know?

(Random trivia only dorks know)

What would they do in a sticky situation?

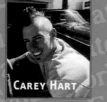

ENICH HARRIS

"I'd probably just blow my nose in the napkin then wipe my hands on the tablecloth. Yeah right...sweeeeet."

CAREY HART

"All I gotta say is, break a few along the way. Makes life fun. Stay away from casts, though."

DARIAN BOYLE

"I am woman, hear me roar! I just like to smile,wink, then smile again. That usually works."

CHARLIE BETTENCOURT

"Uhhh, well...let me tell you. It goes something like this...actually it's uhhh..."

Viva la with "Martha" Robert Earl

floral footwear

This is a no-brainer.

All you do is insert a pint glass filled with water into your boot, and place the flowers deep inside.

Instant happiness, without fail, and it might even make your boots smell better.

What you need:

1. snowboard boot
2. pint glass
3. bouquet of flowers
4. water

Added bonus:

If your boots smell like hell (and for that matter your whole place smells bad, thus the flower vase out of the boot), great things can happen with simple steps. If the boots are totally toast, fill with dirt and plant anything you like—the rubber in the boots makes the roots feel all warm and cozy.

No more stinky pinky!

103

CRACKERS

NET WT 1 LB (454 g)

kris markovich:

Did you hear that Kris Markovich skates for Hollywood? Did you hear that Kris Markovich started Hollywood? Did you hear that Kris Markovich owns Hollywood? Did you hear that Kris Markovich broke someone's nose for calling him an art dog? Where the hell have you been, then?

Sure, he's known for his speed and his encyclopedic knowledge of tricks, but Markovich is also a guy who's not afraid to take chances when he's not skating. He went out on a limb to start his very own Hollywood Skateboards, but then he rolled the company out with a series of ads so gnarly that not even Larry Flynt's Big Brother would publish them!

recipe from my dad. It's one of dishes in the whole wide world.

I'd recommend having creamed corn and green peas with biscuits along with your new favorite dish. Also, for a snack try a peanut butter and jelly ham sandwich.

Ritzy Chicken

ingredients

Extra virgin olive oil
Thawed boneless breast of chicken
Salt and pepper
10 to 15 Ritz crackers
1 tablespoon butter
Chicken bouillion (or two crushed flavor packs from Ramen noodles)

what to do

First heat the oil in a frying pan.
Start to cook the chicken and add a dash of salt and pepper.
While the chicken is cooking crush the Ritz crackers in a bowl. Make sure they're ground up to a fine powder.
When the chicken is cooked, add the butter, then the crushed boullion.
Stir the chicken in the mix and make sure it's all covered and coated.
You're almost done—dip the chicken in the bowl of crackers and put it back into the pan to cook until it's brown and crispy.

Bonus Recipe

The Good Stuff Artichoke
12 heaping tablespoons light or regular mayonnaise
12 heaping tablespoons light or regular sour cream
1 4-ounce can mild diced green chiles (for hotter recipe use half diced jalapeños instead of half green chiles)
2 cups finely shredded Cheddar cheese
3 15-ounce cans of whole or quartered artichoke hearts
2 6-ounce jars marinated artichoke hearts (drained completely)

Combine all the ingredients except artichokes in a medium casserole bowl.
Mash artichokes with a fork and stir into the mixture (allow dip to remain chunky).
When all the ingredients are thoroughly mixed together, cover the bowl with tin foil.
Bake at 350 degrees until dip lightly bubbles (23 to 30 minutes).
Stir and serve.
Goes great with Sun Chips.

Shane Dorian

kitchen emergency

farting in the kitchen

1.

plotz

Problem: you loose a pungent fart at the table

2. Warning: do not say "Sweet, more room for Stove Top stuffing."

mmm...

3. Don't invent a humorous story to cover your shame; have one prepared in advance

The N'gani people of, um, Canada consider the breaking of wind to be a cause for celebration...

4. Blame the dog

5. For the love of God open a window

dishwasher cuisine

Believe it or not, this does work. It has been tested, and the fish does get cooked, although in our shoddy dishwasher we had to run it through two whole washes, so you might need to experiment.

First, get your fish all ready. A whitefish is nice (but any type will do).

Then get that baby prepped with some lemon juice and mangoes or basil, or try Benji's recipe on page 184.

Now get some foil and seal that baby up tight—wrap from the bottom and then wrap again from the top. Now you are ready for the fun part.

Place the fish in the top rack of the dishwasher, and shut door.

Turn the dial to do a full cycle. Once it's run its course you'll be ready to eat. No joke. It's a pretty cool way to impress your guests.

But please, don't add any soap.

Additional dishwasher uses:

Grilling cheese

Boiling water (be very patient)

Reheating pizza

Cooking sausages

BODILY FUNCTIONS
this episode:
the burps

Let the belching begin!

When you eat or drink, air bubbles and gas get into your stomach. But all the bubbles can't stay in your stomach. They burst up through the esophagus (the tube that goes from your mouth to your stomach). When there is too much gas in the the stomach, it comes out as a burp or a belch. But you have to be standing or sitting—you can't belch lying down! In some countries, one belches after eating to let the cook know that the meal was good. In America, many people consider belching to be rude. After a belch, it's always nice to say "Excuse me."

Below are some tips to assist you in sharing your belches with others.

1. First, always be prepared. This means drinking lots of highly carbonated beverages. You never know when a social occasion will require your unique input to bring a poignant statement to the topic at hand.

2. If possible, wait until someone asks you a direct question before cutting loose with a loud report. Point at the person casually as you rumble your response.

3. If you are not skilled at producing a loud or a long belch, you may wish to try the Burp and Blow technique perfected by many a surfer, skater, snowboarder, or BMX rider along the way. This involves a quieter, closed mouth belch, followed by the casual blow or wave in the direction of an audience member, much like exhaling cigar smoke, with a tight lipped "o" shape of the mouth. This works best after consuming large quantities of salami, onions, garlic, or even roadkill. Remember, it's not a belch unless it's shared. If a tree falls in the forest and there's no one there to hear it, does it make a noise?

4. Captive audiences are great for sharing your belches. This would include people in elevators and at corporate meetings.

Definition as it appears in *Webster's*:

Pronunciation: ˈbelch

Function: verb

Etymology: Middle English, from Old English *bealcan*

Date: before 12th century

Intransitive senses:

1 : to expel gas suddenly from the stomach through the mouth

2 : to erupt, explode, or detonate violently

3 : to issue forth spasmodically: gush

Transitive senses:

1 : to eject or emit violently

2 : to expel (gas) from the stomach suddenly : eruct

—belch/*noun*

Some European birds and other animals can produce a voice in which air is actively aspirated into the esophagus and then eructated (belched), as many people can do without practice.

Etiquette 101 with *Robert Earl*

Specialty Silverware

crab or seafood fork

grapefruit spoon

lobster and crab leg cracker

oyster fork

bone marrow spoon

Okay, this is just a little awareness page so these babies don't throw ya; just think multifaceted now. You are prepared for anything. Add them to your arsenal of kitchen stuff.

No one can fool ya now, and don't use the bone marrow spoon to pick your nose. Absolutely not.

The utmost gentleman should know the use of each of these utensils. Get some lobster and make sure to sprinkle sugar on that grapefruit in the morning.

(Random trivia only dorks know)

do they know? What is your favorite piece of specialty silverware?

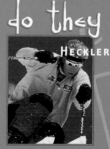

HECKLER

"I'm backing the bone marrow tool. It's weird but I think these things were big in England."

BRIAN DUBIN

"I am going to say the bamboo handled grapefruit spoon. I love grapefruit."

ANDY HETZEL

"Tongs have got to be the best tool in the kitchen, and they are especially good for BBQ-ing."

KAHEA HART

"I really am fond of the crab cracker. It reminds me of the ocean."

111

Is a ruler
Is Australian
Is an international lady-killer
Holds the record for the
highest bomb drop into
a vert ramp (25 feet)

Has lots of animal tattoos
Invented the Ape Hanger
Rules just about anything he
damn well pleases.

Jason Ellis:
APE HANGER

Not happy with being on top of the skating world, Ellis has been known to pick up a mic and host a television show or two, just small things like the X Games.

Like I said earlier, Ellis is a ruler.

But chocolate? Oh, does Jason Ellis ever love chocolate. No doubt that he cannot rule his love for this stuff. We're talking white chocolate, dark chocolate, milk chocolate, chocolate fudge, you name it! If it can rightly be called chocolate, he loves it.

So, Jason has lent us a few chocolate fondue recipes from his years of loving and traveling and basically perfecting the art of fondue. He highly recommends the travel fondue set, which can slip right in your front pocket.

Fondue For Two

Grand Marnier Fondue

2 cups of cocoa powder
1 cup Grand Marnier liqueur (for those of you over 21)
1/2 cup powdered sugar

Put the chocolate, Grand Marnier, and sugar in the fondue pot. Heat gently, continually stirring, until the mix is warm and well blended. Serve with fruit. Bananas are perfect since they can also complement your "Ape Hanger" Ellis move.

Given his love for the stuff, chocolate is the fondue of choice, but here are a couple of recipes that Jason pulled from his secret stash of fondue delicacies.

Suntan Sauce Fondue

3 ounces desiccated coconut
2 ounces creamed coconut, chopped
16 ounces water
2 ounces sugar
4 teaspoons corn flour
5 ounces cream

Drop the coconut in a saucepan with the water, the creamed coconut, and the sugar. Kick on the heat and bring the mixture to a low boil. Cut back the heat and simmer for 10 full minutes. Next, strain the mixture into a bowl, pressing mixture thoroughly to extract all the liquid.

In your fondue pot, blend the corn flour and the cream, then add the coconut mixture you've already made. Let it cook over a medium to low heat until it's all thick and gooey. Then serve it up. This one tastes good with crêpes (which you can buy premade in a store) or even little pancakes, which you can make on your own.

Viva la Fruit Fondue

A big jar of any type of all-fruit jam, raspberry is my favorite (absolutely NO jelly, though—it just doesn't heat up well)
1 lemon
A healthy dash of Grand Marnier

Throw your goods in the fondue pot and let 'er rip! You might want to come up with something special to dip in this one. A nice hunk of fresh sourdough bread works pretty good and so does a croissant or two.

Honey Bunny Fondue

Honey!

Ahhhhh, the Honey Bunny. It only takes one ingredient, so it looks easy, easy, easy. Looks can be deceiving. What the beginner might not realize is what happens when you cut this one loose on an unsuspecting little honey of your own. That's right, an exotic, erotic adventure that you better be prepared to handle. Know what I mean?

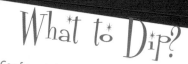

What to Dip?

Confused about what to dip in your fondue? Bread and fruit are the time-honored favorites, but you might want to explore your own exotic fondue sponges. Here's a list of stuff that sounds good with the sweet fondues we're talking about here:

Caramel rice cakes
Chocolate cupcakes
Crêpes
Graham crackers
Homemade biscuits
Macaroons

Mini-flapjacks
Marshmallows
Popcorn
Premade cookie dough
Twinkies
Lickable fingers

paul naude: grommies

ingredients

Bread to toast (of your choice)
Cream cheese
Eggs
Salt and pepper

what to do

Fill a frying pan with 2 inches of water.
Bring the water to a gentle boil.
In the meantime, toast your favorite
bread and schmear it with cream
cheese (be generous).
Crack the eggs in a bowl and drop
them into the boiling water
(a soft, bubbly boil is best).
Let the eggs boil for 2 minutes
and then serve them on your
schmeared toast.
Add salt and pepper to your
liking and enjoy.

These days his job has him at the helm of a great surfwear company.

egg delight

South African native Paul Naude is as core as they come. He started as a board shaper back in the '70s in South Africa, and then he worked and surfed his way around the world, ending up in Southern California. When he's not piloting the Billabong global strategy, you might find him on a company surf trip (Paul has been known to charge the big ones) dropping in with the boys.

Whether we wanted it or not, Paul brings us his South African breakfast delight, and promises that it's so good it will keep you amped all day long, especially if you are charging Tavarua, Todos Santos, or, if you were as lucky as Paul, the hot tub back at the Billabong warehouse. Start your day right...

A good loaf is not just a meal, it's a way of life.

shane Anderson:

There is nothing else that can get you revved up to catch some hospital air. If you want your loaf to totally go off the Richter scale, throw on a little brown gravy. I personally make some mashed potatoes and some sort of steamed veggie to go on the side. I am sure this recipe will change the way you look at ground meat.

(Shane's local mountain is Squaw Valley, USA.)

meat loaf

ingredients

2 1/2 pounds ground beef, venison, moose, or elk
1 egg
1 cup bread crumbs (soft)
1 medium yellow onion, diced
1 packet of French onion soup mix
1 tablespoon Worcestershire sauce
1/4 cup ketchup
4 links hot Italian sausage

what to do

In a large bowl combine the ground meat, egg,
   bread crumbs, diced onions, French onion mix,
   Worcestershire sauce, and ketchup. Take the
   sausage and squeeze the meat out of the skin
   and into the bowl with the other ingredients.
   Knead it all together with your hands until it's
   completely mixed. Then slap it in a loaf pan.
   It's as easy as 1-2-3.
Preheat the oven to 350 degrees.
Pop that puppy in the oven for around 1 1/2 hours
   or until it's cooked.
Now kick back and enjoy the savory taste of an
   American classic.

Dubin

Can't live with 'em, can't live without 'em. X-treme representation—everybody's doin' it these days and the best of the best

X-treme team

Brian Dubin: Ellen's Extreme 900 Noodle Pudding

Brian Dubin makes it happen; from commercials to endorsements he brings it in, a hunter, if you will. Notice his hair—now that is sweet. He brings us the Ellen's Extreme 900 Noodle Pudding, passed down from a long line of Dubins.

ingredients
1 pound medium egg noodles
1/4 pound melted butter
2 extremely jumbo eggs
1/4 cup granulated sugar
1/2 pound cottage cheese
1/2 pint sour cream
1 teaspoon salt
1 teaspoon vanilla
Handful of cornflake crumbs

what to do
Preheat oven to 375 degrees.
Boil noodles "frontside."
Drain noodles.
Mix in butter "backside."
Mix in beaten eggs.
Fold "layback" in cheese and other ingredients.
Top "tailgrab" with handful of cornflake crumbs
    (approximately 900 flakes—count xcarefully!).
Bake until slightly brown (approximately 45 to 50
    minutes).

Eric Zohn: Pasta and Broccoli

Eric Zohn, Business Affairs. He reads them, he tweaks them, and then you sign them—contracts, that is. He brings you Pasta and Broccoli. He had this in a restaurant once and then brought his own version to you.

I created this dish to try to copy a similar bowl of pasta that I had in a restaurant once. I don't remember where, though. My cousin Nicole likes it so much that she tried to order it at Planet Hollywood. They wouldn't make it.

ingredients
1 pound pasta (I like medium shells the best, but ziti is
    the classic to use)
1 or 2 big bunches of fresh broccoli
1 garlic bulb (not just one clove; the whole thing)
A lot of olive oil (your choice)
A handful of shelled and chopped walnuts (optional)
1 can pitted black olives
Parmesan cheese

what to do
Boil your water for the pasta.
Cut and discard the broccoli stems and steam the
    florets just till they turn bright green (1 minute).
    DO NOT OVERCOOK.
Press half the garlic, and slice the rest into thin
    slices.
In a large frying pan, heat the oil and add all the
    sliced and half the pressed garlic. Stir till brown,
    then add the walnuts.
When you add the pasta to the water, add the broccoli
    to the oil and stir. If the broccoli absorbs all the oil,
    add more.
Add half the remaining pressed garlic and stir.
Cut the black olives in half and add to the broccoli.
Add the rest of the garlic and stir.
Grate the cheese.
When the pasta is done, drain it and place it in a large
    bowl, then drizzle the oil from the frying pan into
    the pasta and stir. Then stir in the broccoli and black
    olives.
Place on the table in the bowl and let your guests add
    the cheese to taste.
Mangia!

Ian Kleinert: Lasagna

Ian Kleinert—Literary Agent. Boy, can he read fast. From an Italian neighborhood deep in the heart of NYC, Ian brings us the quintessential lasagna, handed all the way down from his great-great-grandmother from Naples. No wonder he makes stuff happen, it's the Italian heritage. I knew it.

This is my mother's family recipe. I make it, my mom makes it, my grandmother makes it, and my great-grandmother made it. I have tried all of theirs, and can only presume that my great-grandmother got it from her mother in Naples.

Kleinert Jr. standing in for dad

ingredients

4 tablespoons olive oil
10 cloves garlic
3 onions
1 pound hot Italian sausage
1 pound sweet Italian sausage
2 small cans of tomato paste
1 large can of crushed tomatoes
1 box of lasagna noodles
1 very large container of ricotta cheese
1 block mozzarella cheese

what to do

Heat up the olive oil in a big saucepan and turn the heat on medium. When oil starts to heat add the diced garlic.
When THE VERY FIRST piece of garlic starts to brown, add the onions.
When the onions are just about done sauteing, add the sausages.
When the sausages are browned, add the tomato paste and tomatoes. Fill up all three of the empty cans with water and empty those into the saucepan, stirring constantly.

When the sauce starts to solidify, lower the heat. Let it cook for four hours, stirring every half hour to make sure nothing is burning or sticking to the bottom. (A good sign the sauce is done is to take out a sausage and cut it open—if it practically crumbles then it's done.)
Preheat the oven to 375 degrees.
Boil a pot of water to cook the lasagna noodles in. Of course, sprinkle some salt in the water so the noodles don't stick.
When the water is completely boiling add the noodles. Only cook the noodles until they are about half-cooked, that is to say, so that they are still pretty crunchy.
Drain the noodles.
Drizzle some olive oil in the bottom of a lasagna pan.
Spread noodles out so that you have three columns of noodles.
Spread a layer of ricotta cheese on all three columns. After slicing the mozzarella lay three slices in each column. Imagine that there are nine pieces of lasagna, three in each column, each piece gets a slice.
Pour sauce on all three columns. Repeat this process until you are out of ingredients. The remaining sauce should still have your sausages in it . This you eat as a side dish.
You should have about five or six layers per column.
Put in the oven for 30 minutes, let cool, cut into nine pieces and enjoy.

Absolutely do not sign anything.

Read the small print.

Never talk with your mouth full.

And always get someone else to do the work.

how to avoid being a total kook at the beach

7 Simple Tips

Don't put your leash on the wrong foot.
There are few quicker ways into kookdom than the classic leash screwup. If you're a regular-footer (you feel most comfortable with your left foot forward), then your leash goes on your right leg. If you're a goofy-footer (right leg forward), then put the leash on your left foot. The leash always goes on your back foot; it's that simple. And remember, it goes on your ankle, not your wrist.

Don't carry your board with the wax side against your body.
If you don't want to look like you're some dork actor hired for the day to pretend to be a surfer, carry your board like you know what you're doing. The wax side should face out and the nose should be pointed forward. You can carry it under either arm, but follow the two steadfast rules—wax out, nose forward—and you'll at least make it to the water without embarrassing yourself.

Don't put your wet suit on backwards.
Okay, let's get this straight, you're not slipping into a leisure suit. The zipper doesn't go in front. It doesn't matter how many scuba divers with a zipper on the front of their wet suits you've seen on Jacques Cousteau undersea specials. You're going surfing, and in all wet suits made for that glorious pursuit, the zipper goes in the back and that's that.

Don't put your leash on before you walk down the steps and out to the beach.
Not only are you making it harder to get where you need to go, but you're also risking the unparalleled humiliation of tripping over your leash along the way. Save the risk for when you're actually surfing—wait until you get to the water's edge to put on your leash. And for Christ's sake, get it on the correct leg.

Don't put your board on the car the wrong way.
Put your board(s) on the car's rack with the wax side down and the fins at the front. Forget any aerodynamic theories that may make you do otherwise, unless you want to signal the world as you drive down the road that you are indeed a kook.

Don't wax all the way to the tip of the nose of your shortboard.
Does the front of your board look like you're supposed to put your foot up there? Keep the first 18 to 24 inches of your board wax-free. If you're putting a foot up there, you're better off slipping off.

Don't wear your wet suit around for the rest of the day.
Alright now, let's get this straight, it's not an "outfit." Sure, it may have some cool surf company's name and logo, but they made it for you to surf in, not to walk up the street and drip beans from your Taco Bell burrito on. When you're done surfing, change out of your wet suit.

Etiquette 101 with *Robert Earl*

Fondue for You

Since our ladies' man Jason Ellis has prepared a wide variety of fondue dishes and described their results, I felt compelled to lay down the laws of fondue (to further your cause of impressing everyone, including your mother).

The beauty of fondue is its simple sophistication. Your basic dip-and-drip method is in effect whether you're dipping meat or chicken into oil, a chunk of bread into cheese, or a luscious piece of fruit into chocolate.

The item is secured to a long fondue fork, then transferred to your plate by pulling it off with your regular fork. Then with that same fork, down the hatch. Dripping is totally cool, just don't use your best linens.

Don't put the long fork with food into your mouth.

Don't reach over someone after you've just dipped that piece of steak into the hot oil— the result could be painful.

fondue fork

fondue pot

sterno

> Fondue is the true lovers' delight. Whether it's hints of honey, essence of chocolate, or just good old meat, you can't beat the thrill of dipping and gingerly placing the delectable treat into the mouth of a loved one. It's worked time and time again with our noble swordsman Mr. Ellis, so go get that fondue pot and let her rip. Your guest or guests will be pleasantly surprised. Just remember not to point with your fondue fork.

do they know?

(Random trivia only dorks know)

How do you tell which fondue fork is yours?

SPF

"Well, I think you just keep it in front of you until you're done eating."

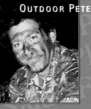

OUTDOOR PETE

"Fork-shmork. I usually just stick my fingers straight into the cheese. Picked that up from my daughter Georgie."

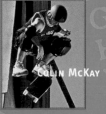

COLIN McKAY

"All I know is that when it comes to the fondue, I watch Ellis's every move. It hasn't failed yet."

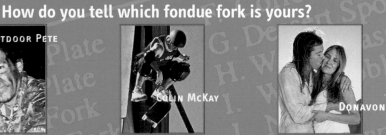

DONAVON

"If I'm with Petra we just share. It doesn't really matter."

121

X-iquette

Don't blow your nose at the dinner table. Also, when everybody's food is on one check, make sure to include your part of the tax and tip when you throw down your money.
That way, you won't all sit there for ten minutes wondering why you're ten bucks short!

Life can be a bowl of cherries oR sour grapes depending

on how you look at things. If the coffee's fresh, then it's all good. Riding bikes for 20 years has been up and down and an all-around treat for me, the good and bad flavors have left me wanting more and more and more. In a strange way it's a lot like the food you choose to eat. Sometimes you can eat the right things and sometimes you can eat the wrong things. Nobody tells you what, when, where, or how to eat, and the creativity is endless if you use your mind. Whatever the case may be, don't hold back when you want to pig out on the Eggo Extravaganza.

extravaganza

Where did it come from?
My wife, Madona, pulled it out of her ear, dude!

What's your favorite food?
Is coffee a food? It is for me! It's the Breakfast of
Champions, and actually does help you "break fast,"
especially when you're running late.

Do you eat anything special before a demo or a show?
Hopefully not my own words. Usually I just run
it on empty.

ingredients

1 Leggo-My-Eggo waffle
Your choice of ice cream (I like vanilla
    bean or chocolate brownie fudge)
International Delights coffee creamer
    (hazelnut or chocolate cream)

what to do

(Pay close attention now.)
Toast the waffle and spread a little
    ice cream on it.
Dump the coffee creamer on top of that.
Eat it up and go back for more.

how to tricks vocabulary

a

Air: Any time you're not on the ground. More is better.

Air-to-Fakie: Any trick in a half-pipe where one rotates 180 degrees or more in an uphill direction.

b

Bail: Ejecting from your board or bike mid-trick.

Barge: To ride, skate, surf, or snowboard in an unauthorized place.

Back Side: The part of your body or board that isn't the front side; for tricks this is when the back foot sweeps behind the skater/surfer/snowboarder/biker.

c

Coping: The top edge (lip) of a mini ramp, vert ramp, pool, or quarter pipe used for grinding—usually made of steel or concrete.

d

Da kine: A very relaxed version of "whatever."

f

Fakie: A term for riding a board the reverse way from how you would normally. Sometimes called switchstance.

Fifty-Fifty: To slide or grind the board parallel to the coping.

Front Side: The part of your body or board that isn't the back side—the part facing any obstacle. For tricks this is when the back foot sweeps in front of the skater/surfer/snowboarder/biker.

g

Gap: A store with lots of boring, unfashionable clothes; the space between the takeoff and landing in a trick.

Goofy Foot: The stance on a board when your right foot is in the forward position.

Grind: To eat or to slide on a rail, coping, or other stationary object.

Grinds: Food.

h

Half-pipe: A generally U-shaped ramp that has a flat section between the two vertical surfaces. Has sent more kids to the hospital than go-carts, minibikes, and chain saws combined.

Handrail: A railing—is used as an obstacle to slide and grind down, or fly over.

Heel Edge: The edge of a board that the heel of the foot rests on on the back side.

l

Locals: Guys who'll kick your ass and slit the tires on your mom's car.

Lip: The edge of any obstacle that a skateboarder rides. On ramps, the lip usually is completed with coping. On a bank or curb, the square or angled corner is the lip.

m

Manual: To balance or ride on either the front or rear wheel(s).

n

Nose: The front of a board.

r

Regular Foot: Not goofy; i.e., standing with your left foot in the forward position.

Revert: An added twist to any trick.

s

Shaka: The secret handshake of the brotherhood of idiots.

Shredding: Getting gnarly, brah.

Slam: A hard fall usually accompanied by swear words and a trip to the hospital.

Sleepahs: Flip-flops, flow-ho's, thongs, etc.

t

Tail: The back, or rear, of a board.

Toe Edge: The edge of a board that your toes point toward.

***Thrasher* Magazine:** The Ozzy Osbourne of extreme-sports magazines.

Transition: The curved section of a vert ramp or half-pipe that occurs between the flat bottom and the vertical walls.

v

Vert Ramp: A half-pipe with an attitude. Vert ramps are at least eight feet tall and have vertical sections near the top and flat bottoms.

Test

Whoa...now this is heavy, but what is it?

a) McTwist
b) Face plant
c) Haakon flip
d) Death

(Answer on page 194)

Kevin

A part of Kevin Robinson has been in the riding

scene since the early '80s. When Kevin started riding he was lucky to tip the scales at 80 pounds, about as much as one of his arms weighs now. Thanks to his dedication and strong will, Kevin maintained a strict diet, trained in martial arts, and of course rode his bicycle.

After many years of touring, doing shows, riding with friends, and pushing his riding to new levels, injuries were inevitable. Kevin decided to dedicate himself to weight training…building his temple (his body) to withstand the attacks of many a foe (or the flat bottom of a vert ramp). When you see Kevin around these days, don't offer him any chicken or turkey, 'cause he won't eat it. Also, don't call him a chicken or a turkey or he'll make you eat what he likes to call a "knuckle sandwich."

"I'm a pretty healthy eater. So I try to maintain a high-protein, high-carb diet. The rule of thumb is to take in a gram of protein per body pound. If you weigh 180 pounds, take in 180 grams of protein. I don't eat deep-fried food or food high in saturated fat, but I do like to cheat once in a while and have my Uncle Paul's Chocolate-Chip Pancakes.

"Before an event I have a high- carb, high-protein meal (your body uses carbs as energy). Make sure you have it at least three or four hours before your event, then right before your event take in some simple carbs like fruit (your body absorbs simple carbs faster than complex carbs). Good for quick energy. After the event find your friends and let the party begin!"

robinson: tuna pasta

ingredients

1/2 ounce angel hair pasta
1 can white albacore tuna
Olive oil
Mild Cheddar cheese

what to do

First make sure you're wearing your chef hat! Cook the pasta. **(If you don't know how to cook pasta, then just go make a sandwich.)**
Drain the tuna well. Mix the tuna and the pasta. Mix it well!
Add some olive oil to the mix to keep it from sticking together.
Add your desired amount of Cheddar cheese. Heat in the microwave for about 1 minute or until the cheese is melted. **(If you don't know how to use a microwave, then you're an idiot!)**
Put it in your favorite bowl. Give it one last mix and eat. I like to add a side of mild steamed broccoli.

...don't call him a chicken or a turkey or he'll make you eat what he likes to call a "knuckle sandwich."

Andrew Crawford:

The recipe is called Turkey Ball.
I have to give full credit to the founder and inventor of Turkey Ball, the legendary Rob Morrow.
This recipe is not for the weak-hearted; if you live off of fine wine and expensive restaurants, get lost! This hearty meal is from the depths of poverty and reeks of the days of scraping together enough money for a Snickers bar after a day of snowboarding on a clipped ticket.

Where did it come from?
The legacy behind the turkey ball is almost unbelievable. I was on my first photo shoot for Morrow Snowboards with Todd Richards and Rob Morrow. I was very nervous, to say the least. On the first morning, we gathered around the kitchen table and made lunches for the upcoming day of shreddin'.

I proceeded to watch Rob, the owner and founder of Morrow Snowboards, in much dismay.

He was mashing chunks of turkey and bread into a big ball, combined with mayonnaise and mustard. The finished product was a ball about the size of a grapefruit made from bread, turkey, mayonnaise, and mustard, gently squeezed into a Ziploc sandwich bag. I asked him why he did that and the answer was simple: "Whenever I get hungry I can just dig into my coat pocket, take out my turkey ball, and have a bite. A turkey ball never falls apart in your pocket like a turkey sandwich would." From then on, I've never questioned the turkey ball again. Over the years I've added my own little twists to the recipe. Remember, this recipe is all about function before fashion, and if you are bold enough to carry a turkey ball, chicks will dig your confidence!

turkey ball

Remember only one thing when making this wonderful entrée: Function before fashion! The turkey ball is a finely tuned machine that will propel your energy level to astronomical proportions, and even though it isn't cute or popular, it will always give you a warm fuzzy feeling.

ingredients

Turkey slices (usually 2 or 3)
2 pieces of bread
Mustard
Mayonnaise
4 saltine crackers (optional)
1 Ziploc sandwich bag

what to do

Cut the turkey and bread into little pieces and then take them in your hands and mash them together like nobody's business.
After a ball is formed, much the size of a grapefruit, take your finger and push a hole in the ball.
Once a nice hole is burrowed into the ball, squeeze mustard and mayonnaise into the hole.
When the hole is filled with mustard and mayonnaise, remash the ball again for proper mixing of ingredients.
(OPTIONAL) If you want, you can crush some saltines and mix them in with the bread and turkey for a crunchy texture.
Place turkey ball into the Ziploc bag and into your pocket.
YOUR DELICIOUS MEAL IS NOW COMPLETE!
I know that turkey ball isn't a babe magnet or a macho meal, but it sure does get the job done and fill you with pride and memories. I would like to give a special thanks and credit to Rob Morrow: Inventor and Founder of the Turkey Ball Association for Kids, and the Turkey Ball Donation Program for Inner-City Youth.

cheese guide

muenster

american cheddar

Favorite all-around cheeses. Used in sandwiches, casseroles, soufflés, and creamy sauces. Flavor varies from mild to sharp. Color ranges from natural to yellow-orange, texture from firm to crumbly.

How to serve
With fruit or crisp crackers on a snack or dessert tray.

bleu, gorgonzola, roquefort

Compact, creamy cheeses with blue or blue-green mold. Sometimes crumbly. Mild to sharp flavor. (Stilton is similiar, but like a blue-veined Cheddar.)

How to serve
Crumble in salads, salad dressings, dips. Delicious with fresh pears or apples for dessert. Blend with butter for steak topper. Spread on crackers or on crusty French or Italian bread. (And for those of us old enough to drink, these cheeses are excellent when stuffed in a giant Spanish olive and served in a vodka or gin martini.)

bleu

brie

brie

Distinctive sharp flavor, pronounced odor.

How to serve
As dessert with fresh fruit. Be sure to eat the thin brown and white crust.

cottage

Soft, mild, unripened cheese; large or small curd. May have cream added.

How to serve
In salads, dips, main dishes. Popular with fresh or canned fruit.

cottage

edam, gouda

Round, red-coated cheeses; creamy yellow to yellow-orange inside, firm and smooth.

How to serve

Great with grapes and oranges. Bright hub for dessert or snack tray. Good in sandwiches or crunchy salads, or with crackers.

swiss

Firm, pale yellow cheese, with large round holes.

How to serve

First choice for ham-and-cheese sandwiches, fondue. Good in salads, sauces, or as a snack.

mozzarella, scamorza

Unripened. Mild-flavored and slightly firm. Creamy white to pale yellow.

How to serve

Cooking cheese. A "must" for pizza, lasagna; good in toasted sandwiches, hot snacks.

muenster (mun´ster)

Mild to mellow flavor, creamy white. Medium hard, tiny holes.

How to serve

In sandwiches or on snack or dessert tray. Good with fresh sweet cherries and melon wedges.

You've read it, you've used it as birdcage liner, you've probably even caught your mom trying to throw it away, but you just won't let her! Not your collection of "America's Favorite Birdcage Liner" aka *Happy* magazine. For years this scrappy So-Cal surf/skate mag has flown well under the radar of the big guys like *Surfer* and *TransWorld* and developed a cult following all its own.

alibaba:

You know that *Happy* magazine just wouldn't be that if it weren't brought to you by its founding father and chief lunatic Alibaba.

Ali, where'd you come up with this one? Is it part of your heritage?

I left home pretty young—in junior high school— and since I was pretty much the only kid who had his own place, my pad was the hangout for the wayward youth in the area. So early on I learned the skill of taking whatever I happened to have in the house and making it into something delicious. Well, not always delicious, but at the very least edible. As long as you've got some eggs on hand, there's usually enough other junk lurking in the fridge for a good old frittata.

Any words of wisdom from Alibaba's kitchen?
Remember, any fool can take a chick out to dinner, but cooking for a girl at your home shows her you care, and you're already halfway to where you want to end up at the end of the evening. Play some soft music (Chet Baker or Nina Simone has always worked for me) and you're one step closer to a night of love.

OUR BIGGEST ISSUE EVER!
MORE SURF!
MORE SKATE!
MORE MUSIC!
MORE SEX!
CORINN! BARES ALL FOR HAPPY

OJ NAMES REAL KILLER
SHOCKING PROOF SURFING MONKEY DID IT!
HAPPY
HAPPY GOES UNDERCOVER
COSTA MESA'S SECRET SEX CLUB
EYEWITNESSES TELL ALL
WHO GOES THERE... AND WHAT THEY DO!
EXPOSED! "Our Gay Secret Life"
EG'S LIPOSUCTION SCANDAL!
SECTOR NINE STAFF BRO TELLS ABOUT HIS BRUSH WITH DEATH!

132

"oh my" frittata

ingredients

1 onion
1 clove garlic (minced)
Extra-virgin olive oil
1 Italian squash or zucchini (thinly sliced)
All, some, or a few of the following: mushrooms, peppers,
    artichoke hearts, sun-dried tomatoes, asparagus tips,
    tomatoes—use whatever you've got lying around.
6 eggs
Salt and pepper
A handful of cheese (different cheeses give the whole
    deal a different taste—try something safe like
    Cheddar or Jack for the first go-round)

1 big frying pan

what to do

Start it rolling by chopping the onion and dropping
    it into the big frying pan with the garlic and olive
    oil over medium heat. Next you'll want to get
    into chopping and adding veggies. Start with the most
    crisp and work down to the softest one. So you'll start with the zucchini and end with
    the mushrooms—like that. The beauty is that in the time it takes to chop each one
    the others are cooking.
As you add veggies, keep the burner on a medium-high heat and keep stirring.
As the veggies cook, crack and beat the eggs in a small bowl with a little salt
    and pepper.
After all the veggie-type stuff is in the pan and cooking and starting to get
    soft, add the eggs you've just scrambled all at once. Once the eggs have
    had a few minutes to cook and you can see that they're starting to gel
    up, stir in the cheese. Turn the heat down after you add the cheese
    and keep lifting the entire egg deal with a spatula to keep the
    frittata from sticking. Once the eggs and cheese and veggies have
    hardened up enough that you can flip the thing over, give it a flip
    with a big spatula—that is, if you can't do the impressive swish-
    and-flip maneuver like a short-order cook (see sidebar).
Once you flip the frittata you should let it cook for a minute
    or two longer, being careful not to let it stick to the
    bottom of the pan. Then cut a nice big triangle out
    of it, shred some cheese over the top, and
    even add a dash of red pesto sauce if
    you happen to have some on hand.

Supa Chef Sidebar

Flippin' eggs or pancakes or just about anything else
with a spatula isn't for prime time. If you're cooking for
friends or that special lady, you need to show some
skills in the kitchen. So learn this trick and remember
it's all in the wrist.

Swish the pan around in a clockwise circle so you break
the eggs loose in the pan. Make a controlled flip of the
pan using only the strength in your wrist. Make a
strong move and continually adjust the height of the
pan to control the rotation of the eggs.

Especially when you're learning, the trick is to pull the
move over the floor, not the stove. This way, if you happen
to miss, your dog can clean up the mess while you
have a laugh and get right back into it with a new one.

nate wessel: mystery

Where does the recipe come from?
It came from my neighbor Marilyn. I'm not sure where she got it, but Marilyn and my mom share little cooking secrets all the time, you know how the ladies are.

Who did you first make it for and where?
Actually, the first time I had it was in fifth grade. It was some special occasion for my brother. But I fell in love with it, so I'm stealing the recipe from my mom. It is only for pretty special occasions, seeing as how it takes six or seven hours to make.

What's your favorite food?
It's a dish called Protein 2000 in a restaurant in Austin called "Veggie Heaven."

Do you eat anything special before an event or demo?
I try to eat small, like a banana or a granola bar. It's not good to eat a lot before you ride. If you eat a lot, your body uses all its energy to digest, which will make you tired. And that's not what you need when you're about to roll in and do some ridiculous run!

meat

ingredients

Mystery Meat Marinade
1/2 cup Worcestershire sauce
4 ounces sippin' whiskey
(Black Velvet is my favorite)
4 teaspoons sugar

Mystery Meat
1 whole beef tenderloin

Béarnaise Sauce for Mystery Meat
2 packages of Knorr Béarnaise sauce
1/4 cup white wine
1/2 cup sour cream
1 to 2 tablespoons tarragon
1/4 cup powdered sugar
1/4 cup salt

what to do

Go ahead and mix up the Worcestershire sauce with the whiskey and the sugar to make a tangy brown marinade. Marinate the meat for between 2 and 6 hours, turning it every 30 minutes.

While your meat is marinating fire up the grill and make the Béarnaise sauce by following the simple directions on the envelope. Then soup it up a little by adding the white wine and sour cream. When you're finished with that, use a whisk to blend in the tarragon.

After it has soaked up as much flavor as you can stand, pull your meat from the tangy brown marinade. Then, to prevent your meat from burning on the grill, roll it in a mixture of 1/4 cup powdered sugar and 1/4 cup table salt. Do this right before grilling.

Cover the meat with tinfoil and grill for about 35 minutes over medium heat, flipping it every now and then so that it cooks evenly.

Slice up your meat INTO THICK SLICES, top it off with our souped up Béarnaise sauce, and eat.

135

Beans Levine

When hunger attacks, blow it away with a burrito.

A burrito page? you might ask. Well, the fact of the matter is—we needed a digital camera for a day. By some gift of God, we met Beans Levine and because we ended up using the camera three weeks, I promised him a page for his Burrito Journal. He even got photos. Yes, this is what happened, so let this be an inspiration to check out all your local burrito eateries. Now we have an Official Burrito Correspondent, and Beans broke down a few of the finer burritos around the La Jolla Community. Remember, no two burritos are exactly alike, and Beans should know; being from California he has eaten plenty.

So, without further ado, here's Beans and a few words. Look for Beans coming to a town near you. You'll either smell him or hear him, if you know what I mean.

The "Burrito Ultimo" from Baja Fresh

This charbroiled chicken burrito mixes grilled peppers, onions, and rice with generous portions of melted cheese, melding the ingredients to create a perfect package. The age-old question "Which bite is sweetest, first or last?" has been argued for hours over this burrito. With its sweet grilled peppers and fresh salsa baja, this "Ultimate" burrito lives up to its name.

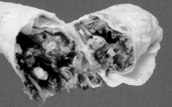

Carnitas Burrito from Porkyland

With a name like Porkyland, this is the place to come to get *carnitas*. The delectable treat is overflowing with some of the most tender pork imaginable. You and your belly will be happy after this meal. The succulent pork *carnitas* will melt in your mouth.

Blackened Fish Burrito from Wahoo's Fish Taco

If you're craving fish, this is for you! Blackened mahi mahi nestled between layers of crisp lettuce, cabbage, and tomato leave a light and filling taste. The fresh fish is expertly seasoned and blackened for maximum taste.

Shrimp Burrito from Fred's Mexican Café

The black beans and shrimp really hold this monster burrito together. Filled with a host of other ingredients such as rice, tomatoes, peas and carrots, this burrito has a distinctive taste and will not leave you hungry. Black beans and rice make this a very filling meal.

"Surfer Gigante Burrito" from Bahia Don Bravo

This incredible vegetarian burrito is packed with flavor! Featuring a whole wheat tortilla, lettuce, potato, salsa fresca, guacamole, sour cream, cheese, black beans, and rice, this burrito is a surfer favorite. The killer size of the burrito gigante leaves it in a class of its own.

Bean and Beef Burrito from José's Courtroom

Here's a portrait of a burrito in its most classic and elegant form—take beans and beef, add some salsa and cheese, and you have a burrito masterpiece. The refried beans and beef mingling with pools of cheese create a sensational taste.

Grilled cheese

ingredients

1 tablespoon butter
3 to 4 ounces American, Swiss, Cheddar, Velveeta, Kraft slices, or whatever have you
2 slices bread
A few drops of water

what to do

Now what you want to do is get out the 10-inch skillet we talked about earlier. Get this baby on medium heat and coat the bottom with some good old butter. Then what you want to do is spread the cheese across the bottom slice of bread.

Then butter the other slice. Now build a sandwich butter side up.

Once the butter in your pan starts sizzling, lay her in. After 3 to 4 minutes, it will be golden brown. Now flip the butter-up side to meet the pan.

About two minutes into this, drop a few drops of water into the pan and cover the pan with a lid. This will get a little steam in there to really melt that cheese. So, so good. And ready to eat!

Have fun! This is an all-time classic you will need to learn and practice so you have it perfected to show your kids.

Bonus Tip

Add a thinly sliced piece of ham. Or even better, asparagus left over from last night's dinner with a tomato. It's super sweet. Add something different each time and you could eat a grilled cheese sandwich every day of your life.

kitchen emergency
dinner guest is choking

Problem: dinner guest choking

Caution: do not ki... choking victim in... buttocks

STOP CHOKING!

Seconds count. Do not pause to fondle breasts

Bottom of Ribcage

Perform Heimlich maneuver on choking victim

Etiquette 101 with *Robert Earl*

Top 10 Dining Mistakes

1. Speaking too loudly
2. Playing with your hair, picking at your face, touching your head.
3. Using your cell phone at the table.
4. Bad posture.
5. Elbows on the table? Absolutely not.
6. Picking your teeth or your butt.
7. Chewing or talking with your gullet open.
8. Pushing the bowl in front of your neighbor when you are finished.
9. Eating too fast. Slow down. Enjoy.
10. Leaving anything on the table (this includes the cell phone you won't be using).

There are tons of others, but if you can remember these you'll be in great shape for any company.

There's probably more than ten but we'll keep it simple. In typical Letterman fashion, here's the top ten list of dining mistakes. And remember, it all else fails resort to K.I.S.S.—keep it simple, stupid. You can't lose. Like a squirrel in winter, just pack in knowledge and it will keep you warm and fed all season. Everybody loves somebody with great manners.

do they know?
(Random trivia only dorks know)

Have you ever encountered a dining mistake?

SHANE ANDERSON

"Whoa, whoa, whoa. The top ten mistakes what? I hardly ever make mistakes."

PAUL NAUDE

"Well, once when I was in South Africa, I saw a shark and it was gray."

KRIS MARKOVICH

"Dining mistakes? What are those? Just eat the Ritzy Chicken and smile."

TODD RICHARDS

"Rarely do I make mistakes, unless I am skating or sometimes in the pipe. Other than that, Powerade rules."

todd Richards:

TR is what those close to him like to call him. Nothing like the '98 Olympics in Nagano for our man TR: first in the Olympics and first out. Whether it's on snow, on the vert ramp, or in the kitchen, TR is totally extreme (but as of late, he's been extremely busy with his new son, who's busy consuming a lot of baby food).

Todd Richards may be the best damn looking rider on the hill, but when he needed to put his wife under his spell, his looks and his signature Wet Cat maneuver were of no use. Nope, he resorted to a trick that no woman could say no to: one extremely romantic night in the kitchen. Like so many moves that he gets credit for, TR would love to lay claim to the All Mashed Up (aka Hot Bean Mexican Salad), but the truth of the matter is he stole the recipe for this gem from his mother-in-law!

So, take two lessons from Todd Richards: Win your ladies in the kitchen and always, always take a few tips from your mom.

Hot Bean Mexican Salad

ingredients

Dressing:
1 medium jalapeño,
   seeded and minced
1/2 cup lime juice
1/4 cup olive oil
1/2 teaspoon salt

Stuff:
1 head Romaine lettuce, chopped
1 tomato, diced
1 avocado, diced
1/2 onion, thinly sliced
1/2 cup Monterey Jack, shredded
1 can of black beans
   (drained and rinsed), heated
Crushed tortilla chips

what to do

Toss the lettuce, tomato,
   avocado, and onion.
Pile on the cheese, then the hot
   black beans.
Crush a handful of chips
   and sprinkle them on top.
Combine all the dressing
   ingredients and pour
   on copious
   amounts.

✦Serve with Margaritas!

Bam margera: flaming

Wooo-ha!

Wait a minute,

Booger Stew? No way. "You can do better than that," I said to the Jackass jester. So Bam came through with something that almost can't be topped—wholly rice balls from France. Who would have thought that Brandon C. Margera even had time to cook? Between CKy videos, pulling off his latest Jackass stunt, teaching Arto Saari how to drive, moving into the new house he recently bought for his family, filming a genuine Hollywood feature, and, oh, his addiction to the band HIM. Yep, the guy's got a lot of stuff going on.

So, between making a leap off a 50-foot-high bridge with nothing more than an umbrella to slow his fall and getting pulled over in his Black Audi A4, Bam has graced us with this unconventional recipe. Hey, when your favorite food is a toasted bagel with mayo, lettuce, and tomato, there's not likely to be much you can tell people about your cooking abilities. So Bam gave us something extra special. Although we don't condone it, you can actually pour gasoline on these babies and light them on fire and huck 'em at your friends! Just the thing when you're looking to start an ambulance-worthy food fight.

"I never but I once a

rice balls from paris

ingredients

1 cup brown rice
1 onion, finely chopped
1 garlic clove, crushed
1 tablespoon olive oil
1 carrot, grated
1/4 cup thinly sliced celery
1/2 cup broccoli florets, cooked
1 tablespoon sun-dried tomatoes,
  chopped
2 teaspoons miso
2 teaspoons sweet chile sauce
1 tablespoon sunflower kernels
2 tablespoons toasted sesame seeds
2 tablespoons wheat cereal
  (extra sesame oil for deep frying)

what to do

Cook the rice, drain well, and leave it to cool. Gently fry the onion
and garlic in oil until soft. Drain the oil and mix all the ingredients
together into balls.

cook
usually eat out
day on average.

In the kitchen with Robert Earl

pantry basics

When You're Stocked, You're Stoked!

Absolutely Mandatory:

Beans: Get 'em canned for easy eatin'.

Crackers: Mix with peanut butter and you've got a meal.

Dried herbs: Basil, bay leaves, chili powder, cinnamon, dill, nutmeg, oregano, paprika, crushed red pepper, rosemary, sage, tarragon, thyme. These can get you high in the right combination.

Flour: White is all right, my friends.

Grits: Good for breakfast, lunch, or dinner.

Honey: Drink it straight.

Hot chocolate: For those cold, lonely nights.

Hot sauce: From the basics such as Tabasco and Cholula, to the more arcane like Dave's Insanity and Nuclear Hell, these are easy to lift from restaurants.

Jell-O: Sometimes it's actually better than nothing at all.

Ketchup: Let's face it, ketchup makes the world go round.

Kool-Aid: Makes any drink taste good. Try it in milk.

Mac 'n' cheese: In France it's called pasta.

Marshmallow sauce: Liquid love.

Mayonnaise: A less glorified version of liquid love.

Mustard: Excuse me, do you have any Grey Poupon?

Olive oil: Extra-virgin, ya heard?

Pasta: At a buck a pound you can't have enough.

Peas: Generally suck, but are cheap and sometimes that's good enough.

Pork Rinds: Deep-fried hog fat, yum!

Ramen: At ten for a buck you're always in luck.

Rice: Brown, white, whatever… it's all good.

Salad dressing: Universal taste enhancement in a bottle.

Soup: Campbell's, of course. Andy Warhol is sweet.

Soy sauce: Makes anything taste good.

Sugar: White and brown for sure; granulated and confectioner's are optional.

Teriyaki: Makes even the most horrible leftover taste okay.

Tomatoes: Keep a few cans on hand for pasta or mac 'n' cheese.

Tortillas: You can't live without those Mexican muffins.

Tuna: Packed in spring water.

Vegetable oil: Doubles as love lube in a pinch.

Vinegar: Balsamic, white wine, red wine, rice wine—they all come in handy.

Pretty Mandatory:

Artichoke hearts: Good for pizza, pasta, and egg dishes.

Capers: Tasty little salt bombs, good for pizza and tuna salad.

Coconut: Good for ice cream and Asian food.

Dried fruits: Great, but generally pretty expensive.

Mushrooms: Yummy, dirt.

Olives: A must, for cocktail hour.

Pesto sauce: Looks like snot, tastes way, way better.

Sun-dried tomatoes: These are expensive; steal 'em from Mom's.

sliced finger

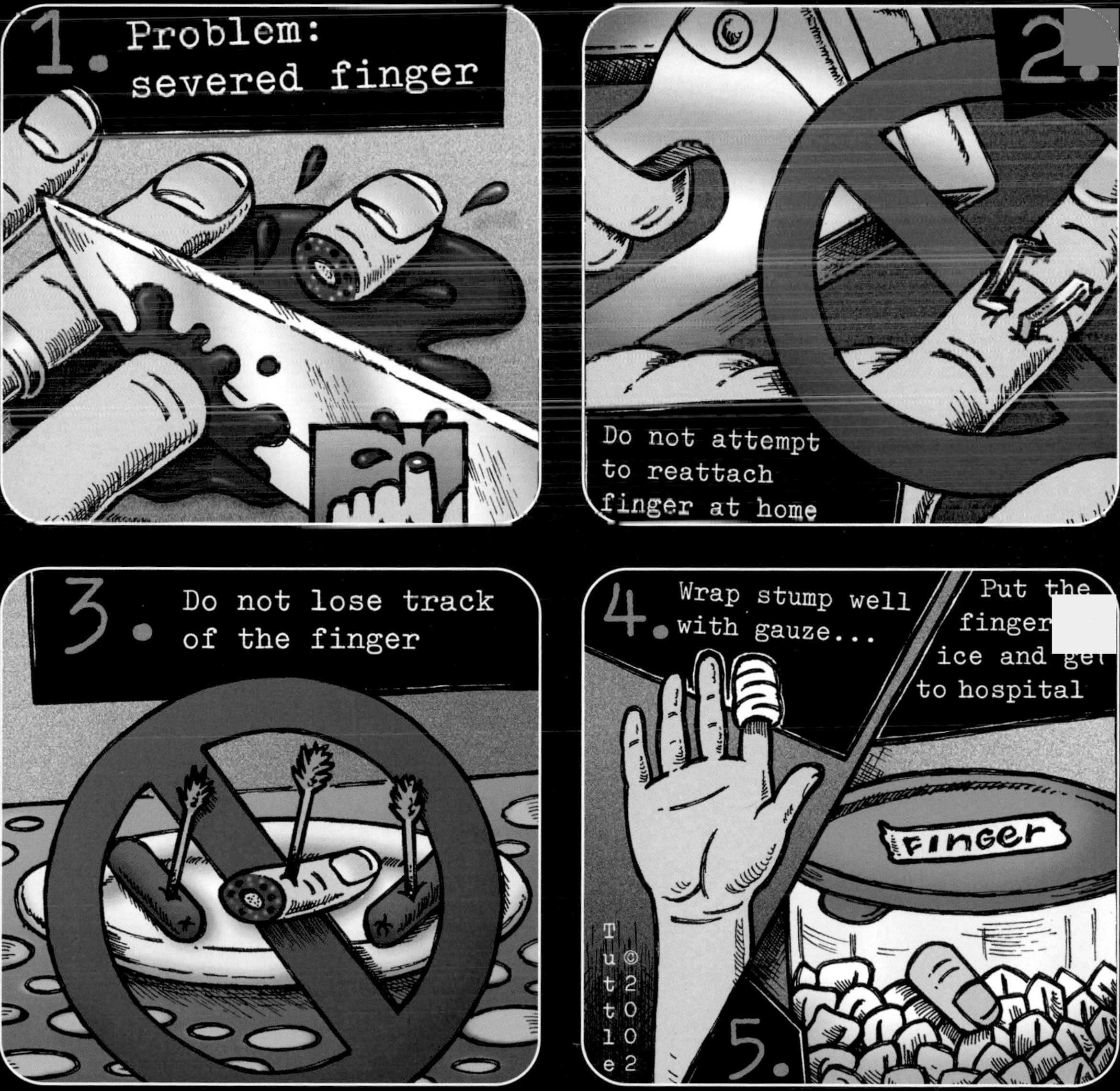

how to *grip tape*

Step one:

The first thing you'll need to do before replacing skateboard grip tape is to get all your stuff together. You will need a screwdriver, razor blade, and grip tape, along with the skateboard you plan to grip.

Step two:

If you want a strip cut out of your grip (so you can see the top graphic, or just to look cool) use the straight edge to cut that now.

Step three:

Peel the tape from its backing.

Step four:

Starting in the center of the skateboard, press the grip tape down.

Step five:

After all the tape is down, use a skateboard wheel (or your thumb) to make sure all of the air bubbles are out.

Step six:

Use the screwdriver to rub a nice little edge along the skateboard.

Step seven:

Use the blade to cut the grip tape along the line you made with the screwdriver. (Always cut away from yourself.)

Step eight:

Use the scraps to smooth the edge along the sides of the board. Put your trucks on and go skate.

146

viva la with "Martha"

Robert Earl

skater's delight

Alright, realistically almost everyone has a skateboard these days. You use it to skate to class, you use it to skate to school, you use it to hang with your bros; now you can use it to score with the ladies. No joke, the skateboard can now be used for more than getting your skate on.

It might sound a little funny but I swear this angle will totally work. Just check out Alex holding up the skate platter.

Just imagine swinging by the store after school or on your way home from the park, grabbing some cheese and crackers, setting up the skate platter, and impressing the girl of your dreams. There is no way she will ever forget this maneuver, I promise.

This is one of my favorites. I mean, you skate to the beach and you cannot lose with this tasty treat. Plus the presentation is probably more worthy than a 10 stair.

What you need

Simple, sweet, and economical
A skateboard
A white linen napkin (or your white T-shirt)
A baguette or French bread
Brie cheese
Grapes and an apple—you are set.

What to do

Now you can serve or be served, whatever your fancy, but nobody is going to turn down a presentation like this.

Take the skateboard, cover with the white linen napkin, place cheese, bread, and grapes on the deck, and *voilà*— you're in business. Serve to your favorite girl or boy and you are sure to leave a great first impression.

Go on now, give it a try. What have you got to lose?

Added bonus:

Basically, when you have impressed the pants off your gal, you can just play it all cool and skate away. Or if she completely dogs you, you can also skate away. It works pretty well. This little trick basically has a 96% success rate, and if you are fairly buffed and want to show off your abs, that's when you can use that nice white T-shirt as the foundation for the skate platter. As well, think of it for your next party. Have your butler try out the skate platter—it will serve him well. Good luck, and now get out there and go for it.

Who dropped the loaf?

147

enich Harris:

Enich Harris
does it all.

He surfs, skates, snowboards, and is the man who has been behind the scenes managing all the action-sports pros for over ten years. Now, as the director of marketing at Billabong, he actually spends more time on the road than ever. Last summer it was the Peel Wheel Tour that had Enich tailing Andrew Crawford and Kevin Jones in Crawford's souped-up Z28; next summer it could be anything.

Where'd this recipe come from?
Javier, my next-door neighbor. He's the most classic guy ever.

Who did you first make it for and where?
On a family vacation. There were like 50 guests and it was the first time I had ever made it. I went huge!

Got a favorite kind of food?
Mexi all the way. Is there anything else in Southern California?

X-iquette

After dinner change your pants before they blow out from overindulgence. Let's face it, after a big meal no one is in any kind of condition to see your butt crack creepin' out of your drawers.

BBQ peaches

ingredients

2 ripe peaches
1 carton Breyers vanilla ice cream

what to do

Cut the peaches in half and remove the pits (the results are better when the peaches are on the riper side, so try and plan ahead for your weekend BBQ).

Throw the peaches on the grill. (Make sure you clean the grill before throwing the peaches on. Salmon or filet mignon char does not go well with peaches!)

Grill the peaches for approximately 10 to 12 minutes (the riper the peaches, the less time they take to cook).

Flip the peaches regularly while grilling.

The peaches are ready when they appear to be soft and mushy.

Scoop 4 bowls of Breyers vanilla ice cream and throw the hot-off-the-grill peaches on top.

Serve to 4 soon to be very happy guests!

I also want to send out props to all my neighbors, Morey, Markoos, Woody, and Javi for helping me hone my BBQ skills. Especially Javi, whose recipe I am taking credit for. Without you guys my BBQ would not have seen the miles it has. Thanks for all the good times and memories!

149

colin mckay:

What good would Canada be without the pure, mouth-watering joy that is **Canadian bacon?**

Professional vert skater Colin McKay took a few minutes to introduce us to something **guaranteed to prove that great things come from Canada.** In tribute, we give you the Canadian Bacon Vert Burger.

Out on the circuit, Colin's even been known to fire up the grill and treat his friends (and a few lucky fans) to the ultimate north-of-the-border burger. And while the coals are heating up, you need to keep your eyes dialed closely, 'cause if you're lucky Colin just might show you a couple of his famed dance moves.

vert burger

ingredients

3 cloves garlic
Bundle of chives
2 eggs
3 pounds of lean ground beef
1/2 pound Canadian bacon
1 package of sesame buns (Colin likes the big buns)
Sliced Cheddar cheese

what to do

Chop garlic into fine pieces. Then chop the chives into even finer pieces. Combine the two piles of fine pieces in a small dish.

Next you'll want to get a big old mixing bowl (Colin has been known to use his helmet, but for the health and safety of your guests it's not recommended). Crack the eggs and drop 'em in the mixing bowl.

Then add the ground beef and mush together with the eggs. Next add all of the chopped elements and mush a little more, combining everything completely. Don't forget a pinch of salt, a dash of pepper, and a little bit of love.

After mushing the beef, eggs, garlic, and chives together, break the huge ball o' beef that you'll have into nine equal parts. Take those nine mounds of meat and slice each one in half, right across the middle, making matching top and bottom pieces.

Now insert the tasty bacon/cheese center that is the taste-bud-popping secret of every Vert Burger: On each of the nine bottoms, slap a slice of cheese and a nice thin slice of Canadian bacon. Then bring each of the nine tops back together with their mate and *voilà*, your Vert Burgers are ready to feel the fire.

Before you drop the Vert Burgers on the grill, make sure there's a pile of glowing hot coals with good heat radiating off it just so. Then on the burgers go.

Cook 'em up just like a regular burger, flipping them every few minutes so you're sure the tasty bacon/cheese center is cooking evenly. When your Vert Burgers are just about finished (you'll know because the center won't be totally pink), toast the buns, and then bring the burgers and buns together in tasty union, and enjoy.

Be careful not to make them *too* good, though. You don't want a bunch of clowns coming over to the ramp every weekend.

This is fresh tuna. Make certain you get the "sashimi grade" stuff. Otherwise, it may taste like, well, tuna.

barbecue basics

The Only 10 Things You Need to Know!

Get Organized: Before you so much as strike a match, make sure you've got all the ingredients that you need and that you have as many items as possible right near the grill. Once the fire is flyin' it's too late to make a trip to the store.

Keep It Clean: A clean grill is a happy grill, and a happy grill is a hot grill, and a hot grill cooks better. Use a wire brush to remove the burnt residue from the grilling surface before every 'cue.

Build It Right: Get your BBQ off to a good start by building the fire correctly. Use the right amount of fuel and only use lighter fluid when necessary.

Get It Hot: If you want your meat to have a crusty exterior and a juicy interior, you've got to get the coals glowing hot before you let the meat hit the grill. The ideal temperature for grilling meat is a full 500 degrees.

Start Off with Easy Meat: Beginners should get things going with a pack of hot dogs and a few pounds of burgers. Then graduate to chicken breasts and fish fillets before you try a steak. Maybe someday you'll step up to a rack of ribs.

Let Your Meat Thaw: Red meat should be at room temperature before it hits the grill. This will give the meat better flavor when it cooks.

Cook Your Meat, Don't Burn Your Meat: There's no reason to cook with a big flame going on the grill. Let the coals burn down to a glowing mass in the bottom—glowing coals are hotter than burning coals and they cook without charring the food.

Show Your Meat Some Love: When you're manning the grill, don't stab the meat with a big, long fork. No, my friend, turn it nice and easy with a good pair of tongs or a long-handled spatula. This keeps the flavor sealed inside.

Separate Your Meat: Once meat is coming off the grill, don't put it back on a plate with raw meat or even on a plate that once held raw meat. Messing with raw flesh on a hot day is begging for a case of diarrhea-causing salmonella.

Little-Known Facts

The original charcoal briquettes were developed in the 1920's by auto magnate Henry Ford, who combined starch with charcoal scraps used in his auto plants.

The first gas-fueled BBQ grill was sold in 1961.

The word *barbecue* is thought to come from a word that Spanish conquistadors picked up from natives in the Caribbean, which they then brought to North America.

About 75 percent of all U.S. households own a barbecue. Something like 60 percent of all barbecues are used year-round.

According to the BBQ Industry of America, there are 2.6 billion BBQ "events" in America every year.

FOOD for thought

with *Robert Earl*

bomber balsamic marinade for chicken

1 cup balsamic vinegar
1/4 cup water
3 tablespoons paprika
2 tablespoons kosher salt
2 tablespoons lemon pepper
1/4 teaspoon marjoram

Blend all of the ingredients together and chill in the
refrigerator for a few hours before dropping your
chicken into the mix.

killer cajun beer marinade for beef

2 cans of beer (the cheaper the better)
2 tablespoons kosher salt
1/2 cup good olive oil
1 tablespoon finely ground cayenne pepper
1 tablespoon rice wine vinegar
1 tablespoon prepared horseradish
1 tablespoon onion powder
2 tablespoons lemon juice
1 tablespoon garlic powder

Blend all of the ingredients together and refrigerate
them for a few hours before adding the beef. Be sure
to put some on the side to baste your beef with while
it cooks.

dry rub (settle down)

2 tablespoons salt
2 tablespoons sugar
2 tablespoons brown sugar
2 tablespoons ground cumin
2 tablespoons chili powder
2 tablespoons black pepper
5 tablespoons Hungarian sweet paprika
7 tablespoons Hungarian hot paprika
2 tablespoons granulated garlic

Blend all of the ingredients together really well and
rub them on the meat before dropping it on the grill.
The longer the dry rub is on the meat before cooking,
the more the meat will absorb the flavor.

side dishes

BBQ beans
Black-eyed peas
Bean salad
Brunswick stew
Celery with peanut butter
Egg salad
Fruit salad

Guacamole
Deviled eggs
Dirty rice
Mac 'n' cheese
Grilled corn on the cob
(or any other vegetable
you can think of)

Grilled potatoes with onion
Hush puppies
Jell-O with fruit in a mold
Jalapeño corn bread
Macaroni salad
Onion pie
Potato salad

Potato chips
Red beans and rice
Salsa
Sweet coleslaw
Not-so-sweet coleslaw
(aka Yankee Coleslaw)

selema masekela:

Host of the year, the voice of action sports, Mr. X Games Selema Masekela, or as you know him good old Sal.

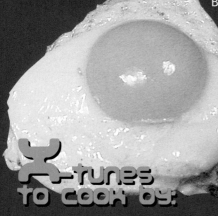

Between awards shows, X Games (winter and summer), and the Tony Hawk Gigantic Skatepark Tour, you'll find Sal chillin' at his spot in Encinitas, California, just cooking away. When we caught up with the dreadlocked man he was actually on his way out the door, off to emcee another comp or skatepark demo.

Just as Sal was rushing off, he told us to get with him another time for a few cocktails and some culinary science. Well, as luck would have it we never got back with old Sal, but on our visit we did manage to lift one of Sal's infamous mix CDs that was lying on his counter. So, at least we know what he likes to listen to when he's cooking up a batch of his legendary Ghetto on the Fly Eggs.

X-tunes to cook by:

1. Hugh Masekela–
   "Grazing in the Grass"

2. Coldplay–"#5"

3. Nas–"One Mic"

4. Stevie Wonder–
   "You Are the Sunshine"

5. Joni Mitchell–"Woodstock"

6. John Coltrane–"Like Sonny"

7. Ghostface Killah–
   "Supreme Clientel"

8. Brand Nubian–
   "Don't Let It Go to Your Head"

9. Black Rob–"Whoa!"

10. Michael Jackson–
    "Don't Stop til You Get Enough"

ingredients

small pot of water
2 eggs
2 slices of white bread
Salt & pepper

what to do

Fill the small pot with water, drop it on a burner, and crank the stove on high.
Carefully drop the eggs directly into the water.
Now you've got 18 minutes to wake up, shit, shower, shave, and get yourself where you need to be before the eggs are done.
By the time you pull yourself together those two eggs should be ready to pull out of the water. Crack the shells with a few taps on the edge of the counter and peel off the hard coating. Put some salt and pepper on those dogs, swallow them in one bite, and go handle your business.
Shit, shower, and shave, 18-minute eggs and garnish with dry toast, but no jelly or butter because you have to keep it gangsta—that's how we do it.

ghetto on the fly
EGGS

155

Bodily Functions

this episode: the farts

Flatus—Ah yes, the Latin word for *wind*.

In this case, it's the wind that howls from the depths of your bowels.

Death, taxes, and farting—three things we all have in common. Sure, your girlfriend might tell you that she doesn't fart, but she's lying! Absolutely everyone passes gas. Studies by flatologists (scientists who study farts and farting) show that most human beings pass an astounding 2 to 8 cups of gas per day. The most likely difference between you and your girlfriend is that she doesn't choose to advertise her bowel-powered bagpipes in the same way that you often do.

What's in your farts?

Farts are composed of gas—gas that in other instances can be lethal or toxic. The average fart is composed of carbon dioxide, hydrogen, methane, nitrogen, and oxygen. The methane in your farts is the same kind of "natural" gas that people use to cook or heat their homes with every day and is one of the reasons that you can actually light your farts on fire. While this type of pyrotechnics can be good fun on a lonely Friday night, we don't recommend trying it yourself.

Because the gases contained in your farts are highly toxic and potentially dangerous, a human's sense of smell has evolved to detect them at extremely low levels. That's why even the tiniest of toots is enough to get you busted.

Here are some tips for keeping your gas output low:

*Avoid bubbly drinks like soda and beer.

*Eat slowly and chew your food well to avoid swallowing air.

*Eat regularly and don't snack between meals.

How to hide the smell of your farts:

There's always the old lighting-a-match trick that is said to not so much combust the smell of a bad fart as cover it up. Otherwise, there are some foods, such as parsley or yogurt, that are known to produce good-smelling gas. Let's not forget the age-old ploy of blaming it on the dog—as good a reason as any to keep a critter around!

Things not to eat before a date: beans, broccoli, garlic, cabbage, eggs, onions

GUARANTEED TO MAKE YOU FART

Apples
Bagels
Beer
Bran
Cucumbers
Dried apricots (and other dried fruits)
Kale
Milk and dairy products
Mushrooms
Nuts
Peas
Prunes
Radishes
Raisins
Soda/Carbonated drinks
Spinach

GUARANTEED TO MAKE STINKY FARTS

Asparagus
Broccoli
Brussels sprouts
Cabbage
Cauliflower
Eggs
Fish
Garlic
Onions

the fart chart

Mmmm, you may get away with a couple.

They're gonna want to know who did this.

This one's a room clearer, a hair burner, a paint peeler.

Mike Vallely

carey Hart: shit on

In a sport where it's a good sign if you're able to move your legs and arms at the end of a run, Carey Hart (aka The V-Town Kid) has a well-deserved reputation as one of the sickest individuals on two wheels. There was the 2000 Gravity Games, where Hart became the first man, woman, or child to ever successfully throw a back flip in competition. So it was understandable that big things were expected of him when he dropped down the takeoff ramp on his Plano Honda 250 in Philly's First Union center at the 2001 X Games. The announcers knew, the crowd knew, and even Hart knew that he had to throw a back flip (aka The Hart Breaker) if he was to live up to his reputation. So he did what any self-respecting MX rider would do: he threw the Hart Breaker, but this time he bailed midflight and ended up with a number of broken bones.

Apparently not happy with one trip to the hospital, Hart, on his first big jump day after his X Games bail, wadded his Honda up on a massive step-down jump in the desert outside of Los Angeles. At least Hart had his latest video, *Good Times with Carey Hart* (a double winner at the Sundance/X-Dance Action Sports Film Festival), to keep him company during his recovery. Oh yeah, and his Carey Hart action figure.

This is a pretty well-known recipe in most places; where'd you learn about it?
Well, the recipe came from when I was a kid living with my dad and we were broke. I was chasing the dream racing my moto as a kid and my dad was just a construction worker so anything that we ate had to be fast and cheap. Even though my dad and I are both doing pretty well, we still like to slum it once in a while and have some S.O.S.

Any hidden benefits in this classic?
The good thing about the dish is that it's really good, pretty healthy, and, best of all, you can feed five people for under six dollars. If you didn't get enough to eat, just drink an extra glass of milk and the potatoes will swell up in your stomach and you'll be full.

You grew up in Vegas. Didn't you hit the buffets for a cheap thrill?
Nah, buffets in Vegas are terrible.

What about all your tattoos, when did that start?
I was 17 when I got my first tat and it was this white trash skull and fire. Sick, huh?

a shingle

ingredients

1 pound ground beef
1 can of cream of chicken soup
1 can of cream of celery soup
1 cup milk
1 box of instant mashed potatoes

what to do

Start the ball rolling by browning the ground beef in a big
skillet. After it's looking fairly well dead and brown, pull it
off the heat and drain the excess grease from the pan.

Next, in the same skillet, add the cream of celery and cream
of chicken soups to the meat. Then add half a soup can of
milk. Blend ingredients together and simmer until the
whole mess is hot.

While you're cooking up the beef/soup mix, you'll want to
follow the directions on the box for making the instant
mashed potatoes. Milk makes them taste better than
water and real butter adds even more flavor.

Once everything seems safe to eat, pour the soup/beef mix
over the mashed potatoes and go to town. A 2-liter bottle
of Mountain Dew helps wash the mix down quite nicely.

outdoor pete

Howdy. Robert Earl calls me Outdoor Pete.

I designed this book.

I like to hunt.

I like to fish.

I like to eat the things that I hunt and fish.

And I especially love my family.

ingredients

Soy sauce	Fresh garlic	Rice wine vinegar	Green onions
Brown sugar	Fresh ginger	Wasabi	

what to do

Mix in a container that will be big enough to hold your meat. I never measure; I just do this by taste, add stuff, taste it, and add more until it tastes right. But do it in this order:

First, pour in enough soy sauce to cover the meat. Next add some brown sugar until it tastes right; you know what teriyaki tastes like, don't you? Then add a bunch of freshly grated garlic. Again, to taste. Then grate some ginger in there. Next, just a smidgen of rice wine vinegar. Careful, don't overdo it, just a teensy bit at a time.

By now it should be tasting just like teriyaki, mmmmmmm yum.

Now the spicy stuff, two choices here: Mix a bunch, I mean a bunch, of wasabi. Fresh is the best, ask your sushi connection. And don't be shy; add a lot of this, because the spiciness kind of cooks out.

Finally, chop up those green onions and toss 'em in.

Ok, plunge your meat into the marinade. Marinate this in the fridge overnight if possible. If it's more of an impromptu shindig, then marinate as long as possible. Tip: massage the marinade into the meat.

An hour or so before you plan on slapping it on the barbecue, take it out of the fridge. You want it to be just about room temperature before you start cooking.

Get the grill nice and hot.

Take the meat out and put the remaining marinade in a saucepan and let it sit on very low heat while you're grilling the goodies.

As for the meat — go as rare as you dare, about 120 degrees on the inside is what I shoot for. You want to sear this and keep the inside nice and red. Try desperately not to over-cook. It will be much more tender and the flavor will actually be less "gamy." And you can always put it back on and cook it more, but you can't go backward, son.

Take the meat off, put it on a platter, and cover it with aluminum foil for a few minutes while you tend to your sauce.

Slice the meat into kinda thin pieces and arrange nicely so when you drizzle the sauce, it looks appetizing.

Take a moment to thank Mother.

spicyaki marinade

"Parko's" straight off of the Gold Coast. The kid's barely old enough to legally drink in the States, but since he became the youngest wild card to ever win a WCT event (J-Bay, 1999), he's joined the crew of young Aussie rulers that's taken surfing's biggest tour by storm in the past few seasons. The pad he shares with fellow surfer and artiste Ado Wiseman looks out on Snapper, one of the great right-hand sand bottom point breaks in the world, so surfing is never far from Parko's mind, even when he's in the kitchen.

But this little story isn't about Parko and his kitchen, it's about Parko and his mobile barbecue or, more fittingly, carbecue. A couple of years back me and Parko and the whole production crew from *Pickled* drove about three hours north of Sydney on a stretch of completely deserted coastline.

JOEL PARKINSON:

The crew, gear, and all the boards were packed into Parko's Land Cruiser. We drove two friggin' miles down the beach so we could set up for some shots at a good break. Like most surfers, Parko's LC wasn't totally up to speed so we were all a little nervous about the whole idea of getting stuck out on a deserted beach with the nearest tow truck a day's walk away. Well, we shoot some great film and we're driving back down the beach when Parko rolls it into second gear and, *boom!*, something under the hood blows.

Seven people in total and nobody freaked too badly—it was like, "Alright, how are we going to deal with this?" Once the steam stopped pouring off the motor, Parko popped the hood and it was clear that the radiator hose had just blown off but, as luck would have it, the clamp that had failed was still sitting on the engine. So Parko, drawing on all of his extreme outback experience, grabs some cheese and crackers from a cooler, puts the crackers on the blistering hot manifold, slices some cheese, drops it on the crackers, tops that with some anchovies and, *voilà!*, outback-style cheese and crackers.

After we all had a little snack and the engine had time to cool down, Parko used his knife to screw the clamp back on the radiator; we filled 'er up with the only drinking water we had, and fired the old LC up. Unfortunately, we were axle-deep in sand, so we had to push the truck the last hundred yards out to the pavement, but it was no big chore with our stomachs full of Parko's gourmet grub.

outback-style cheese & crackers

ingredients

1 package of crackers—saltines, Ritz, FinnCrisp,
  whatever you got
1/2 pound cheese (Cheddar is the easiest to come by,
  but Jack, gouda, provolone, or mozzarella do the
  trick too. Kraft American or Cheez Whiz will do
  in a pinch, especially if you're really going to
  be in the outback, without a refrigerator.)
1 can of anchovies (those packed in olive oil
  are usually the best)

what to do

Crank open the engine of your car, truck, SUV,
  whatever you got. As a rule, the bigger and older the
  engine, the more heat it's going to give off. Drive on over to
  the store to get some supplies: beer, crackers, cheese, that sort of
  thing. Drive home. Pop the hood and feel the heat. Normally, that would all be wasted
  energy, but you're about to make use of all that spent fuel blowin' off the motor.
  For the cheese and crackers recipe, wrap a little foil on the flat, horizontal part of
  the manifold, being careful not to burn your hand. Next lay the crackers, cheese,
  and optional anchovies, in that order, on the foil and let 'er cook. Wait until the
  cheese is just starting to melt and then pull the cracker off the block and enjoy.
  Oh, motor oil and battery acid are not considered to be suitable toppings.

DA - BLACK BEAN STEW

ingredients

Vegetarian version, as prepared by Bob's mom, Dora Burnquist

For the Beans

1 pound black beans, picked over and rinsed
12 cups water
2 tablespoons olive oil
1 large onion, preferably brown, minced
4 garlic cloves, minced
2 twelve-ounce jars of artichoke hearts packed in water
1 8-ounce package of fresh white mushrooms, sliced in half if large
1 pound Italian squash (zucchini), sliced crosswise in 1-inch sections
1 9-ounce Vegi-Deli brand pepperoni, sliced crosswise in 1/4-inch sections
1 tablespoon kosher salt
1 teaspoon freshly ground black pepper
1/2 teaspoon cayenne pepper
1/2 bunch minced Italian parsley

For the Rice

1 tablespoon olive oil
1/2 onion, minced
2 garlic cloves, minced
3 cups jasmine rice, rinsed and drained
1 teaspoon kosher salt
3 cups hot water

For the Collard Greens

12 collard leaves (about 2 bunches), washed and with stems removed
2 tablespoons olive oil
1/2 onion, minced
3 cups jasmine rice, rinsed and drained
1/4 teaspoon kosher salt
1/4 teaspoon freshly ground black pepper

Additional Ingredients

4 oranges, peeled and sliced crosswise
4 tablespoons sesame seeds, toasted and ground

what to do

For the Beans

Bring the beans to a boil over medium-high heat in a heavy soup kettle or Dutch oven, skimming the surface occasionally. Reduce the heat to low and simmer, partially covered, adding more water if the cooking liquid reduces to the level of the beans. Cook until tender, about 3 hours. Stir occasionally.

Heat the oil in a skillet over medium heat. Add the onions and sauté until almost transparent; add the garlic and sauté for 3 minutes more. Add the onions, garlic, and all other ingredients to the beans, and simmer for 30 minutes more. Remove from the heat and add the parsley to the beans. The beans are now ready.

For the Rice

Heat the oil in a medium saucepan over medium heat. Add the onions and sauté until almost transparent; add the garlic and sauté 3 more minutes. Add the rice and salt to the skillet and sauté for 3 minutes, stirring frequently. Add the water, cover, and cook until the liquid is absorbed, about 15 minutes.

For the Collard Greens

Take 6 leaves at a time and roll tightly. Slice crosswise into thin (1/16-inch) strips. Heat the oil in the saucepan over medium heat. Add the onion and sauté until transparent. Add the collard strips and sauté for 3 minutes (until just wilted), stirring frequently. Remove from the heat and add salt and pepper.

Presentation

Serve the beans, rice, collard greens, and oranges on the same plate, sprinkling the ground sesame seeds over the greens.
(Serves 12)

She specializes in big mountain riding, skiercross, and bordercross, but has also been known to get out and surf, windsurf, mountain bike, shag some tennis balls, and spike a few volleyballs. 2000 was huge for Darian because she won the World Extreme Sports Award for best female freeskier. She was unbeatable in skiercross and was crowned world skiercross champion in 1999.

HEAD

Woo-ha! Darian B.
one of the top female extreme
skiers around.

But wait, there's more. Darian is also a model, actress, TV host, and clothing designer. Surf the Internet for a few minutes and you'll find any number of photos of the lovely Darian modeling, acting, and just plain old kickin' it.

sun-dried sensation

ingredients

8 ounces sun-dried tomatoes, finely chopped and in their oil
Artichokes and olives cut in chunks
2 plum tomatoes, chopped
1 cup basil leaves, chopped
2 big cloves garlic, finely diced
2 tablespoons black pepper
1/2 cup extra virgin olive oil
12 ounces Brie cheese (peel off the rind)
1 pound pasta (preferably angel hair)

what to do

In a big bowl, combine the sun-dried tomatoes, artichokes, olives, tomatoes, basil, garlic, pepper, oil, and Brie. Mix it up, making sure that it is evenly stirred.

Cover the mixture with plastic wrap and let it sit on the counter at room temperature for about four hours. Once you've worked up an appetite, boil some water and cook up the pasta. (Bonus Tip: Don't forget to add a few drops of oil to the water so the pasta doesn't stick together.)

When the pasta is starting to get soft (but before it gets mushy) pull it off the stove and drain the water. Next add the big bowl of Brie cheese marinade that you made earlier. The trick with this entire recipe is to pour the marinade on the pasta when it's REALLY hot so the Brie melts right in with the pasta.

If you're feeling extra cheesy and would like to complement the cheese-laden pasta dish with some cheese-laden bread, try this: Take a loaf of French bread and slice it in half. Melt about half a stick of salted butter in a pan and add fresh garlic. Pour the butter-garlic mix on the inside of the bread and top the whole thing with mozzarella and Parmesan cheese. For flavor, sprinkle oregano and parsley on top of the cheese and throw it under the broiler until crisp.

Not for the weak of heart or those watching their diet, that's for sure.

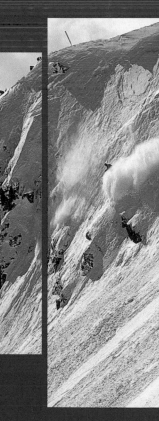

Terje Haakonsen:

He's the Tiger Woods of snowboarding

and like TW, Terje has been known to do what he wants to do when he wants to do it. When he's sick of the half-pipe, he heads for the back country, and when he's sick of the snow, he heads for the sand. Although Terje spends more time on the beaches of Kauai than in his homeland these days, and more time in the water than on the snow, he's still the greatest snow rider who's ever walked this earth—just about anyone will tell you that. Terje may be far from his homeland, but there's one thing he absolutely hasn't forgotten: his family's ancient recipe for a warm and toasty Swedish pretzel.

Check it, it's as simple as a Haakon flip. Right, my friends?

...the greatest snow rider

swedish pretzel

ingredients

1 1/4 cups flour
1 1/2 teaspoons kosher salt
2 tablespoons sugar plus extra to sprinkle
2 tablespoons margarine plus extra to spread
3/4 cup milk
1 tablespoon yeast
Cinnamon
2 eggs
White frosting (optioal)

what to do

Combine the dry ingredients in a bowl.
In a saucepan, melt the 2 tablespoons margarine.
Stir in the milk and heat until lukewarm.
Add the yeast.
Slowly mix the ingredients together and set the dough aside to rise
   for 30 minutes.

Roll out the dough, spread margarine on it, sprinkle on the sugar
   and cinnamon.
Roll it up like a long hot dog, grab each end, and twist in the
   opposite direction.
Lift the long dog onto a baking sheet and form it into a pretzel.
Let rise and brush with whipped eggs.
Bake at 400 degrees for about 20 minutes.
White frosting is optional.

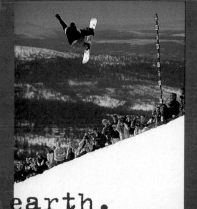

who's ever walked this earth.

In my brief interview with David Paul, who has bailed on the scene in North Lake Tahoe to live the life of an artist/handyman/recluse in his sprawling Reno, Nevada, warehouse, my Lil' Buddy gave me a brief but insightful look into the artfully twisted mind of snowboarding's original renaissance man.

Dave Seoane:

Kicked out of the '83 world cup in Japan for doing an inverted aerial when they weren't allowed, Seaone has always looked at the rules, laughed, and gone about things his own way. With a total of five snowboard films to his credit (producer and director), three signature snowboards, and a 10,000-square-foot warehouse stuffed full of his own furniture and fine art, Dave is ready to take on his next big project: focusing on merging film, metal sculpture, and painting. Be forewarned, something weird might come out of combining the three, he tells us. Who knows what's up his sleeve. Anyway, an inverted aerial in a contest was a little weird the first time people watched him pull it off.

cinema zucchini

An original David Paul.

Rossingnol's first ever pro-model was a Seoane.

ingredients

10 strips of your favorite bacon
1 can of stewed tomatoes
3 baby-arm-size zucchini
1/2 onion, sliced
A handful of mushrooms

what to do

First fry up bacon until golden brown.
Then add the stewed tomatoes, zucchini,
sliced onion, and mushrooms.
Feel free to add your favorite spices such as
garlic, oregano, and cilantro.
After the zucchini is fully cooked, simmer
on low for 15 minutes.
Goes great with your favorite red meat.

175

Willy is one of the technical magicians of the '90s skate movement. He is recognized around the globe for his quiet demeanor and voracious appetite for rails, ledges, and anything urban. Straight from the Philippines (think Cloudbreak), Willy had no problem adapting to American culture except for food. Spicy seafood dishes are a Philippine specialty, and Willy shared a little favorite with me he calls dip, dip, dip, fry. Sounds weird, I know, but if you ever heard Willy speak in his native tongue (for all you trivia buffs, that's Tagalog, which sounds a lot like chirping birds), you'd get it.

willy santos: Dip, dip,

WILLY, WILLY, PAM, PAM. WHAT A DAY.
1999

THE TIMELESS FLAT-TOP MULLET.
1984

SNIP, SNIP, SNIP, BOWL CUT.
1982

THE '80s WERE SWEET.
1987

dip, fry

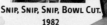

ingredients

1 pound peeled shrimp (medium size)
3 eggs
1/2 cup milk
1 bowl of flour with a pinch of salt
1 bag of coconut flakes
Oil for frying

what to do

Find (and clean if necessary) your hardware.
You may also want to clean and wash the shrimp;
   it's up to you.
Mix the eggs and milk in a bowl.
Mix the flour and pinch of salt in another bowl.
Pour the bag of coconut flakes out onto a plate.
Line everything up so you have your own little
   Nike sweatshop assembly line.
Then, take a shrimp and "dip, dip, dip..." into the first bowl,
   the second bowl, and then into the coconut flakes
   (that's how you get about 20 of these babies all ready to go).
Now you are ready to test your pyrotechnic/arson fetish.
Move your operation to the stove where you have a
   frying pan with about a quarter inch of oil boiling.
Drop the shrimp in and flip them quickly until they're golden brown.
Once the shrimp are cooked, pull them out and let them degrease on a paper towel.
Cool for 5 to 6 minutes and grub, grub, grub, growler!!

Bonus Sauce

Willy's Mom's Ancient Orange Ginger Sauce

1/4 cup O.J. (orange juice, jackass)
2 teaspoons ginger juice (grate 1/2 teaspoon ginger and squeeze)
1 tablespoon chopped fresh cilantro
1/2 teaspoon sesame oil

Place all the ingredients in a small saucepan and mix well.
Bring sauce to a boil .

Willy suggests serving this at the first sign of bubbles—and watch, it happens quickly.

When did you turn pro?
When I was about 16. It was pretty killer. I have ridden for Birdhouse skateboards now for about 14 years. It's been great.

Were you bummed when they poured all the food on you in the movie *The End*?
Well, that was pretty weak, but after going on tour and me being

a little quiet I have to admit I get picked on A LOT! Anyway, it all comes around and I hope that my skating speaks for itself.

how to "jackie chan" sushi roll

ingredients

Seaweed (sushi seaweed)
Rice (medium grain for sushi)
Crab (mix with hot sauce of your choice)
Cucumber
Avocado
4 strips of tuna—cut in 2-inch select cuts
Wasabi
Pickled ginger
Black sesame seeds

what to do

Flip over the seaweed on top of the rice and apply crab down the center.
Next apply the cucumber to the side of the crabmeat.
Roll it up firmly and place on the area.
Apply the avocado and tuna in an alternating pattern—down the spine of your roll.
Wrap with Maki-Su (sushi mat) and pack ends.
Slice roll into eight even parts.
Display the key part of sushi neatly on the board.
Top with wasabi and ginger and sprinkle black sesame seeds on top.

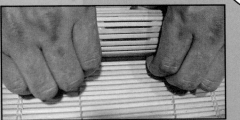

Try this!

If you really mess up, just crumple into a sushi ball and eat like Andrew Crawford's Turkey Ball (see page 128)

What you need

1. wet/damp fingertips

2. clean hands

3. wet rag handy

Etiquette 101 with Robert Earl

The Right Way to Eat Sushi

People in the United States or Europe seem to want to eat their nigiri sushi by dipping it rice-side-down into the soy sauce/wasabi mixture. This is exactly the wrong way to enjoy sushi. Watch a Japanese person—they always dip the fish in the soy and then put the piece of sushi into their mouth whole.

Accordingly, you should never bite into a piece of sushi or sashimi and then put the other half back on your plate. Once you've picked something up, you should eat all of it in one orgasmic bite.

The hot towel (*oshibori*) that you'll be given at the start of your meal should be used to wipe your hands before eating. I repeat, wipe your hands only.

The waiter or waitress is for ordering drinks, soup, or salads from, that's it.

If you want to order sushi, sashimi, or rolls, order those directly from the sushi chef—because he's the man.

As the sushi chef is the man, you may want to bro down with him by offering him a beer or sake. If he's not on the wagon, he'll take it and give you a toast to your health ("Kampai"). Throw him a little shakka.

The Japanese consider it rude to leave rice on your plate at the end of a meal so don't do that.

The sushi chef is just that, a chef. So, don't expect him to deal with your bill, fetch your coat, or take a snapshot of you and your date for posterity. A good sushi chef does one thing really well—cuts fish—and that's it.

> Boy, do I love sushi. I have hunted sushi all over the world. I've had bad fish, I've had good fish, I've had smelly fish, I've had hairy fish, and the worst, a smelly hairy fish. If you travel, here's where you need to go. I am going to have to mention my favorite sushi spot in the world, Sushi Ran in Sausalito, California. Now that's living. Make your way east and there's nothing like Nobu in NYC, and our friends down at Zenbu, in La Jolla, California. Then when you need to do a little riding, make sure to stop by and say hi to Mr. Frittsch and Marty at Yama in Tahoe City. And if you ever make it to London make sure to get into Yo Sushi and check out the robots. With all that said, do not be afraid of sushi. It is good. Try things that you never thought of, like chef specials. And for first timers, the safe route might be to start with Unagi—that's eel—and it's cooked and comes with some sauce. So wash your hands and dig in.

do they know?

(Random trivia only dorks know)

What if your sushi tastes like fish?

PARKO

"I like the fact you can eat it with your hands, and it's super fresh."

TAJ BURROW

"Vegemite and tuna wrapped in seaweed—that's all time, mate."

DAVID PAUL SEOANE

"This strip club directly across from my building, it's pretty cool. Although I've never been."

MIKE V.

"Good. But I really love a nice steak."

morgan stone:

Oh Jeez,

I know you've seen *Tony Hawk's Gigantic Skatepark Tour* on ESPN. Well, you may have wondered who orchestrates all that madness? You've got him right here. This is the man behind the scenes—Mr. Morgan Stone—affectionately known by all on Tour as the great and powerful "Morgazmo."

In the following X cuisine spotlight you will see exactly how Morgazmo earned his moniker, while learning his tried-and-true recipe for turning a one-night stand into a bliss-filled weekend of love!

Study Morgazmo's magnificent and delightful recipe. Learn it well and just wait and see what returns it will bring. Morgazmo didn't get his name for nothing.

No joke, Morgazmo is **The Man** between the sheets as well as behind the camera.

Straight from Morgazmo: "Living life on the road can be very hard on a long-term relationship.... Ask any of my seven X-girlfriends. Eventually you will find yourself with the awkward yet inevitable one-night stand and the morning that follows. So here it is, my secret recipe. This will ease your sleepover partner's nerves and make it a fun-filled morning, and if you're lucky, an action-packed weekend. ***Bon appétit.***"

DUTCH BABIES
...for the morning after...

ingredients

3 eggs
1/2 cup milk
1/2 cup flour
1 teaspoon lemon juice
2 sticks butter
Powered sugar
Fruit (strawberries, blueberries,
    blackberries, raspberries)
Whipped cream

what to do

Mix the eggs, milk, flour, and lemon juice. Whisk until blended.
Preheat the oven to 475 degrees. Grab a pan, preferably 12 x 8 inches.
Put 1 stick of butter in the pan to melt, coating the bottom, then pour in the
    batter.
Bake for 20 minutes.
Melt 1/4 to 1/2 stick of butter in a saucepan (depending on your level of
    cholesterol).
After 20 minutes remove Dutch Babies from oven and pour on butter, top
    with powered sugar.
Layer with the sliced fruit.
Put the whipped cream in a side bowl.
Wake up your unsuspecting date and serve. And if you accidently spill some,
    make sure to lick it up. (If things go well, breakfast could turn into
    dessert.)

Bonus Tips

1. Never kiss and tell.
2. If you have to kiss and tell, just claim you only made out.
3. If you don't look like Don Juan, props are key.
4. Piggyback rides are a guaranteed icebreaker.
5. Even if you are in town for a week, tell 'em it's your last night.

If you are having trouble hooking up, see the "Mookie-Bear" recipe on page 38.

Charlie is a lifer.

charlie bettencourt:

I like to start with a proper piece of fish such as Copper River Salmon.
If you can't find C.R.P., then any good fish market will have some wild salmon for you. This recipe is written for single portions.

ingredients

1 teaspoon olive oil
7-ounce piece of fish
Salt and pepper
2 teaspoons fresh dill
Fresh lemon

what to do

Rub the oil on the salmon and sprinkle it with salt and pepper to taste. Then rub on the dill.

The fish should be cooked over a medium flame. Prepare the grill by rubbing olive oil on it using a paper towel.

Place fish on the grill skin-side up and cook for 3 minutes. Flip and cook 3 minutes on the other side. Flip once more with skin facing up and turn fillet 45 degrees to get those familiar BBQ marks we all love so much.

After placing the fish back on the grill peel off the skin and cook for 3 minutes more on that side. Flip one more time and cook for 2 minutes more, squeezing some lemon on the fillet.

Done.

grilled dill salmon

Charlie is a lifer. He's the guy you run into at a ski resort who spends every day of his life there skiing. He's someone who just couldn't leave—the guy who turned a passion into a lifestyle. Charlie's here to show that this approach can pay off. And it did. Apparently he's eating salmon, he's smiling, he's skiing a lot, and he made it in the book all because he followed his heart.

Here are a few words from Charlie:

"I showed up in Squaw in '80. Things were wide open. No closures and no lawsuits. You could ski anywhere and launch anything. Downhills and G.S. skis ruled the hill. It was a great time to be at Squaw. Even though things have changed from those days, one thing has not—the mountain is still the same and is the training ground for some of the best skiers in North America. History speaks for itself.

"I developed my recipe from my friend who took me salmon fishing when I was living in Southern Humbolt. I would barbecue fresh-caught salmon and camp at Shelter Cove. Then my recipe was dialed in by my friend Gerry Conney, the head chef at Fiama in Tahoe City. He taught me the art of measuring herbs and all about temperature control."

Self-proclaimed: "I have made more successful SNEAKIES out of Squaw Valley than anyone."

Benji Weatherly—a professional surfer and Billabong global team member. He's probably got the best gig in the world—a bon vivant and world traveler, Benji has seen it all. From South Africa to Vive la France he's been pickled, and has he been pickled. Few words are needed for this quiet man.

The bottom line is Benji loves Lindy. Lucky him.

Benji Weatherly:

steamed thai fish

1 1/2 cups water
1/2 cup rice wine or rice wine vinegar
1 tablespoon sesame oil
1/2- to 1-pound fresh halibut fillet
2 cloves garlic, chopped
1 tablespoon fresh ginger, chopped
5 thin orange slices

what to do

Combine water, rice wine, and sesame oil in a covered wok, over medium/high heat.

Next, in a bamboo steamer (very inexpensive to buy at any Asian market), lay the fish (really about any type of fish will work, and in real Thai restaurants they'll use a whole fish). Put a few deep, diagonal slits in each side of the fillet to allow the flavor to seep into the fish. Sprinkle with the garlic and ginger and arrange the orange slices in rows around the fish.

Once the water, vinegar, and oil mixture in the wok is boiling, reduce the heat and fit the steamer over the top of the wok. This may take some chopsticks and some ingenuity, but figure out a method that works for you.

Cook for 15 to 20 minutes. You'll know it's done when it looks like it's going to flake apart. Once the fish is done to your liking, remove the steamer from the wok and carefully transfer it to a serving plate. Garnish with Asian green beans and sprigs of lemongrass and serve with dipping sauce.

Green Onion, Ginger, and Garlic Dipping Sauce
ingredients
2 tablespoons soy sauce
2 tablespoons peanut oil
1 tablespoon chopped green onion
1 teaspoon chopped fresh ginger
1 teaspoon chopped garlic
Pinch of brown sugar

what to do
Basic. You can make this while your fish is cooking.
In a glass bowl, combine all the ingredients and blend well with a whisk. You can play around with the ingredients you use, trying things like cilantro, cayenne pepper, and fresh orange, to your liking.

viva la with "Martha" Robert Earl

surfboard bliss

Here are some helpful hints for turning a typical beach outing into a day someone will remember for a lifetime. Why? Because that's what it is all about, and I personally want to change your life with this book. So try a few of these out and let me know what happens.

For this Viva La you'll need a beach. It can be a beach on a lake, the coast, at a pond, or wherever else you can think of that's fairly romantic. Or maybe you just wait for that special day you travel to the coast, rent a board, and paddle out for the first time.

First you need a surfboard. A short board will do perfectly for a romantic encounter for two, but if you're thinking group affair, grab the long board and set the table for ten.

Then you're going to need some plates (plastic will do just fine). Try and find a little picnic kit; they have everything—the glasses, plates, and even forks and spoons.

Add a tablecloth (a towel will do just fine, but if you go the towel route, make sure not to use the moldy one that has been stuffed in your trunk for six weeks) and your food of choice. Crackers, fish, bread, cheese, chicken salad sandwiches—the sky is the limit here.

Flowers are a key ingredient as well, as they can be dried and saved for a reminder of the special occasion.

Best time of the day for the ultra sheiky setup is sunset, of course.

Windy days suck.

Rainy days do not work for this setup.

Added bonus:

This can actually be tweaked for a snow setting as well. All you need to do is swap out the surfboard for a snowboard, and make sure you serve hot chocolate and a warm something or other to your lucky date!

wait what why!

Bodily Functions
this episode: boogers

What is a booger made of?

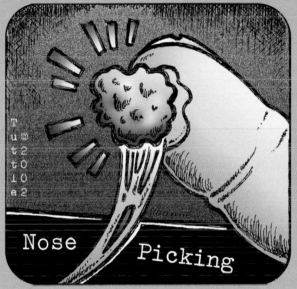

Nose Picking

Definition as it appears in *Webster's*:

Pronunciation: 'bu̇-gər

Function: noun

Etymology: alteration of English dialect *buggard*, *boggart*, from [1]bug + -ard

Date: 1866

1 : bogeyman

2 : a piece of dried nasal mucus

Boogers are mucus (myoo-kuss). Mucus is the thin, slippery material that is found inside your nose. Many people call mucus snot. Your nose makes nearly a cupful of snot every day. Snot is produced by the mucous membranes in the nose, which it moistens and protects.

When you inhale air through your nose, it contains lots of tiny particles, like dust, dirt, germs, and pollen. If these particles made it all the way to the lungs, the lungs could get damaged and it would be difficult to breathe. Snot traps the particles and keeps them in the nose.

After these particles get stuck inside the nose, the mucus surrounds them, along with some of the tiny hairs inside the nose called cilia. The mucus dries around the particles. When the particles and dried-out mucus clump together, you're left with a booger!

Boogers can be squishy and slimy or tough and crumbly, but the truth of the matter is, boogers are a sure sign that your nose is working properly.

Yes, you know it, he could be (and probably is) the greatest athlete on earth. He's the godfather of extreme sports. He's the Evel Knievel for the new millennium. Damn it, he was extreme before there *was* extreme. That's right, from mountain bikes to snowboards, from skis to motorcycles and on to race cars, the Mini Shred has done it all and won it all. What's more, the kid can't quit. Look for him to hop in an open wheel can and blaze to glory at Indy some day.

shaun palmer:

The man from Tahoe's South Shore will tell ya that the key to his success—are you listening?—is that he takes his food seriously. Very seriously. As I have found, you don't ^!%#$ with Palmer when he's near food or he might switch it up and eat you for dinner. Oh, and the ketchup, that was Uncle Randy's idea.

...don't f#$! with Palmer when he's near food or he might switch it up and eat YOU for dinner.

french toast
with ketchup

ingredients

2 eggs
1/4 cup milk
1 teaspoon vanilla
1/4 teaspoon ground cinnamon
2 tablespoons butter
4 slices white bread (you can use Texas-
   style bread, which is about 1 inch thick)
1 teaspoon powdered sugar
Ketchup

what to do

The first thing to do is prepare the batter for the bread. Beat the eggs, milk,
   vanilla, and cinnamon together in a shallow pan. The pan should be shallow, but
   make sure that its diameter is a little bigger than the bread you're going to use.
Warm up the stove to a medium heat. Use a Teflon pan (some prefer a griddle pan).
   Whatever you have, heat some butter so it melts evenly in the pan.
Now you're ready to introduce the bread to the batter, so get your dip on. Don't be
   scared, either!!! When dipping the bread into the batter, make sure that you do
   one slice at a time, both sides.
Put the coated bread into the heated pan or griddle and brown it briefly on each
   side, being careful not to overcook it.
There you go. Now for the final step: a huge, whopping amount of, yup, ketchup.

ridiculous facts

Robert Earl

A cow weighs about 1,400 pounds and eats about 55 pounds of food per day.

An African elephant will eat up to 500 pounds of food a day. Its diet consists of twigs, leaves, grass, and fruit.

Most fish eggs are almost yolkless, since they are laid in water, where food for the unborn fish is readily available.

In 1765, the sandwich was invented by John Montagu, the fourth Earl of Sandwich, who gave the food its name. The earl used to order roast beef between pieces of toast for a snack while he was at the gaming tables, which allowed him to keep one hand free to play while he ate.

Caviar, or fish eggs, contain the same healthful omega-3 fatty acids as salmon.

In 1889, Aunt Jemima pancake flour, invented in St. Joseph, Missouri, was the first self-rising flour for pancakes and the first ready-mix food ever to be introduced commercially.

Celery has negative calories—it takes more calories to eat and digest a piece of celery than the celery has in it initially.

Nutella is a hazelnut spread made with skim milk and cocoa. It is virtually unknown in America, but European children have happily smeared it on breakfast croissants for decades.

Of the 350 million cans of chicken noodle soup sold annually in the United States, 60 percent is purchased during the cold and flu season. January is the top-selling month of the year.

In 1893, Milwaukee's Pabst beer won a blue ribbon at the Chicago World's Fair, and was sold thereafter as Pabst Blue Ribbon beer.

Official FDA guidelines allow whole pepper to be sold with up to 1 percent of the volume made up of rodent droppings.

In 1948, it was common to see carhops serving those who wanted to order food from their car. Harry Snyder of Baldwin Park, California, had the idea of a drive-through hamburger stand where customers could order through a two-way speaker box. Harry opened California's first drive-through hamburger stand, named In-N-Out Burger. Today In-N-Out remains privately owned and has 148 stores in three states.

In 1954, Trix breakfast cereal was introduced by General Mills. The new cereal, a huge hit with kids, was 46.6 percent sugar.

Olive oil is made only from green olives. Nearly the entire crop of green olives grown in Italy is converted into olive oil.

In 1976, the first eight Jelly Belly flavors were launched: Orange, Green Apple, Root Beer, Very Cherry, Lemon, Cream Soda, Grape, and Licorice.

In 1984, Britons ate 41 pounds of beef per person per year, according to the Meat & Livestock Commission. By 1994, the figure had dropped to 35 pounds. In March 1996, "Mad Cow Disease" in Britain lowered the consumption figure even more, although many Britons continued to eat roast beef despite the scare.

"Sherbet" is Australian slang for beer.

"Poached egg" means "egg-in-a-bag," from the French word *poche*. When an egg is poached, the white of the egg forms a pocket around the yolk; hence, the name.

On average, each American consumes 117 pounds of potatoes, 116 pounds of beef, 100 pounds of fresh vegetables, 80 pounds of fresh fruit, and 286 eggs per year.

On average, there are eight peas in a pod.

Food & Wine magazine reported that in Japan squid is the most popular topping for Domino's pizza.

In 1996, Chicken Alfredo was introduced as one of the new flavors of Gerber baby food.

Papaya leaves and unripe papaya have an enzyme called papain that breaks down protein in meat to make it tender. That's why papaya can be used as a meat tenderizer.

The edible fruit of a passion flower is called a maypop.

Paper can be made from asparagus.

In Australia, the number one topping for pizza is eggs. In Chile, the favorite toppings are mussels and clams. In the United States, it's pepperoni.

The fortune cookie was invented in 1916 by George Jung, a Los Angeles noodlemaker.

Per the U.S. Department of Agriculture, Americans are heavily into French fries, eating an average of 30 pounds per person in 1995, more than triple the amount consumed in 1965.

Pizza now ranks as the top fast food in America, but is only number four in Canada, where hamburgers are the number one fast food.

Plain old vanilla is the favorite flavor of ice cream, accounting for 29 percent of all sales.

In the country of Tibet, it's good manners to stick out your tongue at your guests.

Winking at women, even to express friendship, is considered bad manners in Australia.

The custom of serving a slice of lemon with fish dates back to the Middle Ages. It was believed that if a person accidentally swallowed a fish bone, the lemon juice would dissolve it.

credits

Embry

PURDY PITCHERS

Mike Basich: pages 4–5, Tina Basich action and snow lifestyle

Kirk Bender: pages 160–161, Carey Hart action and lifestyle

Big "B": pages 56–57, SPF lifestyle

Big Island: page 12, Dave Mirra action; pages 126–127, action Kevin Robinson; pages 134–135, Nate Wessel action

Mike Blabac: page 32, Danny Way's Christ air action; page 112, Jason Ellis

Grant Brittain: pages 1–2, Mike Vallely lifestyle and action; page 33, Danny Way helicopter; page 66, Bucky action; pages 74–75, Kevin Staab action; page 95, Tony Hawk action; pages 168–169, Bob Burnquist action; page 176, Willy Santos action

Rob Brown: pages 86–87, Mike Parsons spread

Brian Castillo: page 122, Rick Thorne action; page 47, Rooftop action (sequence); page 64, Simon Tabron action

Jeanne Durst: pages 4–5, Tina Basich lifestyle and dining room

Danny DeSanti: dannydesantifoto.com; page 147, Alexandra Elizabeth Harlan bikini model; page 186, surfboard picnic table

Bud Fawcett: budfawcett.com; page 99, Andy Hetzel train jump; pages 188–189, Palmer action and lifestyle

900 Films/Jim Harrington: pages 62–63, Mat Hoffman; page 42, Shaun White lifestyle, action; page 47, Mike Escamilla lifestyle; page 62, Mat Hoffman action; page 67, Bucky Lasek lifestyle; pages 70–71, Brian Sumner; pages 94–95, Hawk portrait; page 122, Rick Thorne lifestyle; page 154, Selema Masekela lifestyle; pages 158–159, Mike Vallely pool

Erik Ippel: page 9, Kahea Hart action

Carol Morris: page 2, Airstream

Jody Morris: page 150, Colin McKay action

Jason Murray: page 87, Mike Parsons lifestyle

Naki: pages 2–3, Donavon action and lifestyle

Scott Needham: snp@snp5000.com: pages 36–37, Shane Dorian; pages 58–59, Luke Egan lifestyle and action; page 74, cover shot; page 83, Taj Burrow; page 85, Mouse's wall shot; pages 106–107, Shane Dorian spread, Dorian bail; pages 164–165, Joel Parkinson action; pages 172–173, Terje action and lifestyle; pages 184–185, Benji Weatherly spread.

Ted Newsome: page 104, Kris Markovich action

Scooter 'n' Riley

Mr. Tuttle

Dave Norehad: pages 18–19, Aaron McGovern; pages 34–35, Bradley Holmes road gap; page 54, Brad Holmes action and lifestyle

John Old: page 49, Steve Caballero action

Embry Rucker: page 129, Andrew Crawford; pages 140–141, Todd Richards action and lifestyle

Aaron Sedway: pages 78–79, Tom Burt lifestyle and action; page 129, Andrew Crawford action; page 174, Dave Seoane action

Shalihe: page 10, Willy's How to Ollie

Jason Shields: pages 40–41, Jimbo Morgan action and lifestyle; page 116, Shane Anderson; pages 170–171, Darian Boyle lifestyle and action; page 182–183, Charlie Bettencourt

Simone: page 14, Peter Line lifestyle

Brian Smith: page 68, Pat Parnell lifestyle

Sweet Pussy Frank: page 6, bread and butter; page 8, Kahea lifestyle; page 11, all; page 16, tuna; pages 29–30, all; pages 38–39, honey bear and Carter; page 97, Hawk-Riley lifestyle; page 99, Hetzel cops

Jan Tanju: page 48, Caballero lifestyle

Jeff Taylor: pages 142–143, Bam Margera

Miki Vuckovich: page 76, Doll shot Staab

Jeff Zielinski: page 61, Rooftop Action roof fall

PURDY DRAWERINGS

Jonathon Tuttle: Every illustration in this book, from farting to chopping off fingers, was done by the Magnificent Tuttle. Portfolio: home.pacbell.net/neddyboy or email: neddyboy@pacbell.net

PURDY WURDIES

Mark Reidy: text editor and wordsmith who made it all happen on the back side, and really loves periods. He's responsible for making the text flow in an orderly fashion, thank the skies above for our meeting at Loews.

Scooter Leonard: special thanks to him for his wonderful words that graced the pages of *X-treme Cuisine*. Scooter is the man and his son Riley is the little man.

Sweet Pussy Frank: for his athlete wrangling and photo shoots. Without him it wouldn't have been possible. He came through in the clutch. Frank, I think I love you.

Kelly Miller: official recipe consultant who helped us through all those metric conversion moments. We are thankful they teach them so well at the California Culinary Academy in San Francisco.

collector's cards

What you need:

1. clean hands
2. scissors

Get out your favorite pair of scissors and cut out these collector's cards! Be sure to keep them handy in your kitchen for when hunger strikes or an opportunity to impress arises.

Answer to the test on page 125: For the average person, the answer is death, but for a legend like Shane Dorian, falling off a thirty-foot wave is just another day at the beach.

ingredients

1 egg
1 shredded Jack & Cheddar
    cheese mix
1 bagel (preferably plain)

what to do

Find a microwave-safe bowl approximately the same diameter as a bagel. "We have perfect-size Tupperware bowls in our house, but I have no idea where they came from."

Crack the egg over the bowl and pour it in. If you manage to not spill any egg outside the bowl or get any bits of shell in it, then you are a Bird Bagel Prodigy. Scramble it.

Sprinkle cheese over the egg, covering the top completely with a thin layer.

Split the bagel and stick it in the toaster.

Heat the egg in the microwave on high for a minute and a half.

Wait patiently—have some coffee or juice. Now is a good time to throw the egg shell away, put the cheese back, and clean the fork you used to scramble the raw egg. Never risk salmonella for haste.

Use the freshly cleaned fork to remove the egg and cheese creation from the bowl and place it on the bagel. Work on the timing of toasting versus egg cooking so that both come out hot (cold eggs are nasty).

Cut the Bird Bagel in half and consume. Eat it in your car if you are in a hurry. Don't forget to pick up a vanilla café au lait or Vanilla Iced Blended if there is a Coffee Bean and Tea Leaf on your way.

ingredients

5 or 6 Weetabix
1 ripe banana
1 jar honey
1 carton milk

what to do

Start by putting roughly five Weetabix in a cereal bowl. Next, select a ripe banana from a bunch, peel it, and slice it into small pieces. I like to peel one side of the banana off and cut it with my spoon while it's still in the other half of its peel. Using the spoon amounts to limiting this whole recipe to one utensil, which obviously saves time when it comes to washing up!

Put the sliced banana on top of the Weetabix and smother it with as much honey as you can stand. Then add milk. I usually like about a half-filled cereal bowl in order to avoid what is commonly called soggy Weetabix! Our motto around here is to Never Eat Soggy Weetbix (NESW), also known as North East South West! Haaaaa.

ingredients

2 pieces of bread (or as much as you can eat)
1 stick butter
1 jar of Vegemite

what to do

Start with a few slices of your favorite bread (mine is a soy/linseed special). Next, toast the bread for as long as you like.

Then, smother as much butter on it as you can possibly feel comfortable with.

Ok, here's the key to top-shelf Vegemite Toast: just thinly spread your Vegemite around your butter-soaked toast. In a lifetime of experimentation, I've found that a small amount of Vegemite spread very thinly works the best.

MIKE V.
WHITE TRASH CASSEROLE

WHITE TRASH CASSEROLE

1 BAG POTATO CHIPS (preferably BAR-B-QUE flavored)
1 PACKAGE MACARONI + CHEESE
1 CAN OF BAKED BEANS OR CHILI
IT DOESN'T get ANY Simpler Than THIS:
COOK The MACARONI + cheese
COOK The BEANS or CHILI
LINE A PLATE w/ A HEALTHY HEAPING
    PORTION OF CHIPS...
ADD The MACARONI + cheese.
ADD The BEANS OR CHILI.
MIX Together AND EITHER EAT w/ YOUR HANDS
LIKE NACHOS OR USE A FORK.

— Mike V.

BAM MARGERA
FLAMING RICE BALLS FROM PARIS

ingredients
1 cup brown rice
1 onion, finely chopped
1 garlic clove, crushed
1 tablespoon olive oil
1 carrot, grated
1/4 cup thinly sliced celery
1/2 cup broccoli florets, cooked
1 tablespoon sun-dried
    tomatoes, chopped
2 teaspoons miso
2 teaspoons sweet chile sauce
1 tablespoon sunflower kernels
2 tablespoons toasted sesame seeds
2 tablespoons wheat cereal
   (extra sesame oil for deep frying)

what to do
Cook the rice, drain well, and leave it to cool. Gently fry the
   onion and garlic in oil until soft. Drain the oil and mix
   all the ingredients together into balls.

ingredients

1 pound peeled shrimp
(medium size)
3 eggs
1/2 cup milk
1 bowl of flour with a pinch of salt
1 bag of coconut flakes
Oil for frying

what to do

Find (and clean if necessary) your hardware.
You may also want to clean and wash the shrimp; it's up to you.
Mix the eggs and milk in a bowl.
Mix the flour and pinch of salt in another bowl.
Pour the bag of coconut flakes out onto a plate.
Line everything up so you have your own little Nike sweatshop
assembly line.
Then, take a shrimp and "dip, dip, dip..." into the first bowl,
the second bowl, and then into the coconut flakes (that's how
you get about 20 of these babies all ready to go).

Now you are ready to test your pyrotechnic/arson fetish.
Move your operation to the stove where you have a
frying pan with about a quarter inch of oil boiling.
Drop the shrimp in and flip them quickly until they're
golden brown.
Once the shrimp are cooked, pull them out and let
them degrease on a paper towel.
Cool for 5 to 6 minutes and
grub, grub, grub,
growler!!

ingredients

1 pound ahi (yellowfin tuna) cut
into 1-inch cubes
4 teaspoons soy sauce
1 cup chopped onion
4 teaspoons chopped green onion
3 teaspoons sesame oil
1 teaspoon sesame seeds
1/4 cup Nori Furikake Japanese
seasoning (optional)

what to do

Place ahi cubes in a mixing bowl, add all other
ingredients, and mix well.
Serve chilled.
Enjoy with chopsticks.

LUKE EGAN
PASTA WITH CABONASI SAUSAGE

ingredients
Cabonasi sausage, thinly sliced
1 whole garlic bulb, chopped
1/2 stick butter
1 pound thick fettuccine noodles, cooked
Tin of peeled tomatoes
Tin of tomato paste
(You can also use Newman's Own
   tomato sauce. Luke highly
   recommends it.)

what to do
Pan-fry the cabonasi on low heat with the garlic and butter.
Now put the noodles, the cabonasi, and the red tomato
sauce all in one big-ass bowl, mix, and serve to the
woman or man of your dreams.

DONAVON FRANKENREITER
PETRA'S STIR-FRY CHICKEN VEGETABLE CURRY

ingredients
2 tablespoons peanut oil
3 garlic cloves, minced
2 teaspoons ginger, finely chopped
1 red onion, finely chopped
1 pound boneless, skinless chicken breasts
   cut into 1-inch chunks
3 tablespoons soy sauce
2 to 3 tablespoons curry powder or paste
   (paste is usually better)
1 cup water
1 cup chicken stock
2 red potatoes cut into 3/4-inch cubes
   (leave the skin on)
2 carrots cut into 2-inch pieces

what to do
Warm the oil in a wok or frying pan (a wok is usually
   better) until it is very, very hot, but not quite boiling.
   Add the garlic, ginger, and onion. Stir and cook for
   approximately 3 minutes or until everything is softened.
   Add the chicken chunks and cook until the chicken is
   white all the way through (you shouldn't see any pink in
   the chicken). Once properly cooked, put the chicken-chunk
   mix into a separate bowl for later use.
Now, in the wok, add the soy sauce, curry, water, stock, potatoes, and carrots. Bring it to a simmer, then reduce the heat
   and let cook for 15 minutes. Keep covered and give it a little
   stir every 5 minutes.
After 15 minutes, add the chicken-chunk mix you prepared
   earlier. Cook for roughly another 10 minutes.
At that point, the sauce will begin to thicken. Be sure to taste
   it during this time because it's your big chance to make any
   adjustments.
From there on, it's off to the races to eat and be merry.
   And remember, a nice large bowl of rice is key, just in case your
   mouth starts to catch on fire from Petra's spicy stir-fry.
   Bon appétit, amigos.

ingredients

Hostess Ding Dongs or King Dons
(as many as desired)
Godiva Vanilla Caramel Pecan
ice cream
Chocolate ice cream with
swirls of golden caramel and
roasted pecans
Creamy peanut butter
Hershey's Chocolate Milk Mix
1 microwave oven
1 big smile

what to do

Warm the Ding Dongs in the microwave for about 25 seconds.
Place the warmed Ding Dongs in the bottom of a bowl, and
add the ice cream on top. Microwave the creamy peanut
butter to desired consistency (the more time, the more liquid),
then add to the dessert. Sprinkle with Hershey's Chocolate Milk
Mix and serve!

ingredients

1 Leggo-My-Eggo waffle
Your choice of ice cream
(I like vanilla bean or chocolate
brownie fudge)
International Delights coffee
creamer (hazelnut or chocolate
cream)

what to do
(Pay close attention now.)
Toast the waffle and spread a little
ice cream on it.
Dump the coffee creamer on top of that.
Eat it up and go back for more.

DAVE MIRRA
THE MIRRA MIX LIGHT

ingredients

1/2 pound pork tenderloin
1/4 cup unsweetened pineapple juice
1/4 teaspoon ground ginger root
1/4 teaspoon red pepper sauce
1 clove garlic, finely chopped
Cooking spray
1 medium onion, chopped (1/2 cup)
1 small red bell pepper, cut into thin strips
2 tablespoons reduced-sodium soy sauce
    or fish sauce
3 cups cold cooked white rice
Chives, chopped for garnish
Soy sauce to your desired amount

what to do

Remove the fat from the pork. Cut the pork into 1/2-inch cubes.
Mix the pork, pineapple juice, gingerroot, pepper sauce, and garlic in a glass or bowl. Cover and refrigerate about an hour before cooking.
Remove the pork from the marinade and drain. Spray a 12-inch skillet with no-stick cooking spray. Heat it over medium-high heat, add the pork, and stir-fry it 5 to 10 minutes or until no longer pink. Remove the pork from the skillet.
Add the onion and bell pepper to the skillet; stir-fry about 8 minutes or until the onion is tender. Stir in the pork, soy sauce, and rice.
Cook about 10 minutes, stirring constantly, until the rice is hot and golden.
Sprinkle with chives; serve with soy sauce.

ROOFTOP
SALSA FA NU

ingredients

2 tablespoons diced white onion
8 Roma tomatoes
2 to 3 tablespoons cilantro, chopped
2 diced jalapeños (no seeds)
2 serrano chiles, diced
1 teaspoon salt (add more if needed)
1 tablespoon lime juice (either from
    concentrate or just squeeze a slice in)

what to do

After you've chopped everything up, put it all in a mixing bowl and blend the ingredients. Try the salsa with a chip and see if you have to add more of ingredients that don't stand out enough.
Cover and refrigerate for a couple of hours. The longer it sits, the more the flavors will blend. I hope it's good; if not, blame Robert Earl—he made me do this!!
Now go jump off a building.

Good job. Now get to the kitchen and start cooking!

Feel free to email me any questions. robertearl@xcuisine.com Have fun and keep cookin'. Bon appétit.

Eddie H. Eppes for being an incredible human. Chris Lillis, my mother, for not abandoning me because I never call. Gerry Lillis for being there for Chris. David Paul, for being a dear, dear friend. Bob Wells for…well, just being Bob. Heather and Matt Ramsey for having the cutest kid in the world, Riley Lorraine. Robert E. Wells Jr. for being super sweet and marrying Himer. Himer for being my #1 fan, always. SPF and Hannah for all the dinners and sleepovers on their couch. Georgie Blue for being Cinderella, Bailey Jane for being Dream Baby, Carol Morris for being invincible. Peter Morris for finding the Hello Kitty panties at 2 am and making this thing happen. Extra special thanks, Pete. I swear I will pay you. Mark Reidy for making it all come together and being the wordsmith from heaven and staying up really, really late and never complaining about my disorganization. Thanks for all the commas and words, Reidy. Yours next. Morgan "Titanium" Stone for his undying support and belief. 900 Films for just being sweet. Matty Goodmanos for being Matty without fail. "T to the O to the N to the Y" Hawk, birdman "the guy," the hummingbird, for being superhuman, kind, and good to all. Joe Sibilia and all his beliefs. The Gasoline Alley Foundation, for keeping the entrepreneurial spirit alive. Claire, Kristen, Kendra, Kayla. For being girls. Uncle Festy and Eileen for being. Reid Strathern for becoming Extreme Reid and Envision Entertainment. Beth of course.

thank-yous

William Morris Agency, Eric Zohn for thinking outside the box and making it all happen. Ian Kleinert for not being scared, and being Italian. Brian Dubin for wearing sweet jeans. Kerry Simon for looking young and being my culinary inspiration. HarperCollins, Josh Behar for his undying support of the project even though I was always late. And I mean always. Thanks, Behar, I owe. Parr, Goldman & Byrne. Tim Parr for being part of the Total Party Network and Annie Rosenthal for marrying Tim. LuLu Parr, for being Tim's daughter, and AJ for being sweet. Alexandra Elizabeth (Alex) for making me completely nuts and being you. Kemp Curley and Tara Davis for almost keeping me organized. Kevin Harrison for being the dirty dog. Transition Productions for flying to Cali for a pitch. Nicole Sanchez for being a sweetheart. Steve Yinger, the yindogger, for being all yindog stylee, and rebeliscious. Wait, whoa. Amy Anderson for leaving the electrician, working very late, and putting up with all the smells. Mike and Chris Pack for the fresh air, starstruck. And Tom. Headhunter Doug for making us late and having white teeth. Harshburglar for being all-beach safety. Mark Muller for being a hunter, and giving me edamame. Tim Johnson for being a sweet sushi chef. Clutch, Jackie Beer for all the special attention. Alibaba and yes, Happy Mag. Kevin Meehan for being super studly. Surfer Mag. Graham Stapelberg for no recipe. Phil Ward for being the milkman—I know Phil a bonzer.

Jared Prindle for always looking good. Activision for being gnarly. Will Kassoy, sorry about the recipe, Will. And David Pokeress. Hubble for being my undying friend. Kerry for never cutting my hair and being buff. The Moosehead Beer delivery girl, Erin Fitzgerald, for being sweet and delivering beer. Billabong for all their undying support. Stephanie Pair at Billabong—Ian, the designer of the year. Tim, and Curly, and everyone else at Billabong. Mike and crew at La Jolla Photo & Imaging. Riley Lorraine for being cute. To every athlete for following their dreams and fighting all the odds, especially all those who took the time to help with the book. I hope this is fun for you to be part of. Everyone and everything that has helped me in any way, thank you. Thanks to the believers and the dreamers. Thanks to MLV, wait, what...his wife, for being patient with him. Heckler for the beer. Big Curtis at Inn by the Sea. Pat, Dorothy, and Jim, for making Pat Pat. Dr. J.A.K. Peterson for missing his wedding. Sorry, thanks for the walk on the beach, Doctor. Big Island for all the last-minute shiiiaaattt. The MGM Grand in Las Vegas for the dollar slot machine that turned my last $4 into $400 during the making of this book. Wait, Wheel of Fortune 25¢ slots and Tim Helion for his fresh perspective at the Deux in Reno. Without you the project would have never been finished. I love you all. Thank you. And thank you to everyone who buys this damn book!